MW00331273

773 - 894 - 3805

The
Other Side

Stephen Shaw

The
Other Side

Copyright © 2014 Stephen Shaw

First published in the United Kingdom in 2014 by Stephen Shaw

Cover art by Deborah Grieves - http://cynnalia.deviantart.com

Publisher and author website and contact details:
www.i-am-stephen-shaw.com

The right of Stephen Shaw to be identified as the Author of this Work
has been asserted by him in accordance with the Copyright, Designs
and Patent Act 1988 (UK) and the Berne Convention for the Protection
of Literary and Artistic Works. The moral rights of the author have also
been asserted.

All rights reserved. No part of this book may be reproduced by any
mechanical, photographic or electronic process, or in the form of a
phonographic recording; nor may it be stored in a retrieval system,
transmitted, or otherwise be copied for public or private use – other
than for 'fair use' as brief quotations embodied in articles and reviews
– without prior written permission of the publisher.

The intent of the author is only to offer information of a general nature
to assist you in your quest for emotional and spiritual well-being. In
the event you use any of the information in this book for yourself,
which is your constitutional right, the author and publisher assume no
responsibility for your actions.

ISBN: 978-0-9928042-1-3

Stephen Shaw's Books

Visit the website: www.i-am-stephen-shaw.com

I Am contains spiritual and mystical teachings from enlightened masters that point the way to love, peace, bliss, freedom and spiritual awakening.

Heart Song takes you on a mystical adventure into creating your reality and manifesting your dreams, and reveals the secrets to attaining a fulfilled and joyful life.

They Walk Among Us is a love story spanning two realities. Explore the mystery of the angels. Discover the secrets of Love Whispering.

The Other Side explores the most fundamental question in each reality. What happens when the physical body dies? Where do you go? Expand your awareness. Journey deep into the Mystery.

Reflections offers mystical words for guidance, meditation and contemplation. Open the book anywhere and unwrap your daily inspiration.

5D is the Fifth Dimension. Discover ethereal doorways hidden in the fabric of space-time. Seek the advanced mystical teachings.

Star Child offers an exciting glimpse into the future on earth. The return of the gods and the advanced mystical teachings. And the ultimate battle of light versus darkness.

The Tribe expounds the joyful creation of new Earth. What happened after the legendary battle of Machu Picchu? What is Christ consciousness? What is Ecstatic Tantra?

The Fractal Key reveals the secrets of the shamans. This handbook for psychonauts discloses the techniques and practices used in psychedelic healing and transcendent journeys.

My friends call me 'regular Joe' and I don't mind. It's probably because I have no huge ambitions. When I was 18, some of my mates went off to college and university to pursue higher education. That never grabbed my interest. A few enlisted in the armed forces to serve and defend the country. Good for them. A couple got married young and started their own business. I wished them the best of luck.

Inwardly I am shrugging and smiling. Nothing really bothers me. I am a regular guy with an ordinary job. You wouldn't notice me. I am the guy who smiles at you in the morning as you order your fancy coffee. Sure, I have a title: barista (from the Italian for 'bartender'), a pretentious word for a coffee-house employee.

What will it be today? Caffè Americano? Caffè Latte? Caffè Mocha? Cappuccino? Espresso? Your wish is my command. 90% of the work involves takeaways, fuelling the adrenaline rush for City bankers and managers. Yep, the people who own these coffee chains. Whatever. They can have the stress. Watching the markets and having early heart attacks; it's not for me.

The part of my job I most enjoy is the sit-downs. Those wonderful people who actually have 15 minutes to spare. What's the rush anyway? Where is everyone going in such a hurry? I take good care of my sit-downs. My favourite clients are those who don't seem to worry about the time. Online newspaper in hand, they casually nibble a croissant and slowly sip a steaming coffee.

Many of my sit-downs are regulars. Though we seldom exchange more than a greeting and a few polite words, they keep coming back. Nothing is ever overtly said … just a silent acknowledgment … an inner smile.

The reason? I have a secret.

If you have a few moments … slow down … take a deep breath … and place your order … I need only a second to look into your eyes and gaze upon your soul. I see your essence. I know what's going on in your life.

This is when I sprinkle my magic. Your cappuccino arrives. What do you notice? A roaring lion amid the swirling white foam? A butterfly rendered from chocolate syrup and froth? An inspiring phrase written with cocoa powder?

Always that moment of hesitation before you sip. You receive the message. My work is done. Goodbye gorgeous coffee art, hello delicious cappuccino!

And that is my life. As simple as it is. Sowing tiny inspirations here, little heart-hugs there. And why not? I have an abundance of joy in me. Perhaps I am a regular Joe but I think I am the happiest person on the planet.

At the end of each day I finish cleaning the tables, pack everything away, and catch the train home. I can't afford to live in the City. Who can? That is the domain of the CEOs, stockbrokers, bankers and rich kids. The sun will go down and they will come out to play. Desperately trying to fill their empty souls with champagne-and-cocaine-fests, sexual flings and tales of market exploits. Bravado and balderdash. That's the world they created. That's the world they live in. It's so pitiful that you don't know whether to laugh or cry.

The train ride takes about 45 minutes. I love watching the ever-changing countryside. It's a moderate climate but we get the occasional flurry of snow. In spring, buds and shoots appear everywhere. In summer the fields turn from green to brown. It's all beautiful. If you truly embrace your surroundings and take it all in, there is so much to appreciate.

A short walk down a tree-lined avenue takes me to our small apartment. We live on the second floor, facing south-west. The building is positioned on a hill and I can see the ocean from my window. When the sun is shining I throw open the shutters and stare at the shimmering waves. What more do I need? Delightful warmth cascading across my skin, fresh breeze caressing my face, birds chirping cheerfully in the tall trees. Absolute bliss.

I glance at the to-do list. 'Take the washing off the line. Peel potatoes.' Better get on with it. She'll be home soon. I walk outside and grab the peg basket. Her white nightclothes are gently fluttering. I reach up and breathe in her delicious scent mingled with soft lavender. Instantly transporting me to the moment she first walked into the coffee-house ...

Three short years ago ... bouncy long blonde hair ... ice-blue eyes ... same height as me ... curves in all the right places. For me, though, it's always the eyes. One glance carries a thousand messages. A leisurely gaze portrays the pages of the soul. Nothing is ever hidden from one who espouses courage and vulnerability.

I feel sad for people who chase 'gorgeous and sexy'. As if muscular shoulders or pouty lips will bring joy to the spirit. Don't get me wrong – Angela is a very attractive woman. But I fell in love with her essence, her inner nature. If you connect to the right spirit, everything else falls into place. It's called making love for a reason, and it's far more fulfilling than random sexual encounters. Once two hearts are deeply intertwined, a profound peace and deep contentment arises.

I have learned that joy comes from making choices based on the heart and spirit. And it's already inside you. Every answer you need is sitting right here. The problem is that our minds are corrupted by all the nonsense propagated by popular media. TV reality shows that promote celebrity lives (as if they need more money or publicity); advertising which uses physically appealing actors and scantily-clad models; the constant titillation of sex and violence in films and television programmes; newspapers and magazines purveying physical beauty and celebrity gossip.

It's no wonder people are confused and empty. Tantalising ghosts are flaunted by powerful persuaders and influencers, whose only real interest is extracting every last cent from foolish spectators. One day you wake up and realise that having a gym-honed body, the latest fashions and the chicest hairstyle *will not bring you happiness*. You cannot catch a ghost. Those are mere illusions designed to sap your hard-earned money.

I hear the front door opening and the pitter-patter of little feet. "Daddy? Daddy?" Ah, the second love of my life. "Ryana, sweetheart, come here." I sweep my gorgeous two-year-old into my arms and hold her tight. Such soft skin. Then I hoist her into the air and gaze into her eyes. She giggles playfully.

"Hi, honey." I kiss Angela on the lips. "Haven't done the potatoes yet. How was your day?"

"The usual," she sighs. "Working for an egomaniac who wants to rule the world."

"Stockbrokers, eh?"

"It pays the bills. Hopefully I am talking sense into him along the way."

"I don't know how you do it."

"I'm not changing careers just because my boss is short-sighted. He doesn't know how lost he is."

"Always trying to help others … That's why I love you."

She rolls up her sleeves. "I'll cook if you bathe Ryana."

"Deal."

We trundle off to the bathroom, turn the taps and unpack the plastic toys. Smiling dolphin, yellow duck, bobbing boats, brightly coloured cubes and orbs. Half an hour disappears amid delighted babbling and gurgling. Carefully wash her hair; always a challenge. Lift her out. Standing beside the bath wrapped in a fluffy white towel. Can it get any cuter than this?

Soon we are sitting at our modest dinner table. Glass-topped, which I like, but we have to take care with our baby. The evening passes with the usual banter, a couple of bedtime songs for Ryana, and quiet reading on the sofa.

When we finally clamber into bed, I draw Angela close for a cuddle. "I'm so glad we are married. You and Ryana are the light of my life." She smiles and kisses me softly. "And you are mine."

Moonlight is streaking through the shutters. My eyelids feel heavy. The mauve-colour walls are soporific. I tug the feather duvet to cover my shoulders. The last thought is always the same: Deep gratitude for a perfect life. I gradually fade into a swirl of fantastical dreams.

* * *

The morning is the usual chaos of alarm clocks, showers, breakfast, dropping Ryana at playschool, catching trains and embracing the hustle and bustle of the City. I tend to wake up foggy and groggy; perhaps that is why I work in a coffee-house. Truth is, I am more of a night owl whereas Angela is an early riser. She is often up at 5am, pottering around the apartment. I seem to need more sleep, barely able to function before 7am. Married life tends to sync your clocks so we usually fall asleep together. Intimacy is worth the sacrifice of my natural rhythm.

Unlock the doors, flip the switches, inspect for cleanliness and presentation, stocktake and orders, morning espresso, lay out muffins and croissants, online newspapers in the rack. *Bam, bam, bam!* The harsh knock startles me. A man with unkempt long dark hair, olive skin, unshaven. I glance at the clock. Ten minutes until opening time. My colleague nods affably, plants the Specials board on the sidewalk and welcomes the customer.

The dishevelled man sweeps in, long coat flaring behind him. Not a City boy, that's for sure.

Broad smile. *I've heard you make award-winning cappuccinos.*

My usual penetrating gaze falters under his confident demeanour. I manage an "Uh huh" and fumble with the chilled milk pitcher. Press the brew button. Wait. Nothing happens. Press it again. My colleague strides over and adjusts the settings. Still nothing. I scratch my head. This never happens.

Roisterous laughter. *Looks like you have a ghost in the machine.*

"I beg your pardon?"

An invisible breeze wafts through his hair.

My name is Michael. And you, my friend, are confronting the most fundamental question in your reality.

I stare at him for a moment then raise my hand. "Give me a few seconds. It's a temporary malfunction."

The air is really still, the ambience strange. I feel light-headed and off-kilter. Come on, don't fail me now. Suddenly a billow of steam erupts and everything is working. I seize control. Adept service is essential. Brew. Milk. Steam. Froth. Steal a surreptitious glance into his green eyes. Shock of light hits me. Feel a bit nauseous. Overwhelmed. Sketch out a radiant sun using cocoa powder and foam.

"Here you go, sir. Newspapers are in the rack."

He disappears to a table by the window. The coffee-house gets a morning rush. I watch him out of the corner of my eye. Not moving, not reading. Sipping an endless cappuccino. Exuding an uncommon peace, a kind of knowing confidence. The hint of a wise smile etched on his rough face.

At 10am he departs. A friendly salute his only goodbye. Intrigued and confused I move to clear the table. Cup still half full. Scrawled across the immaculate white napkin in fine cocoa powder, the words: 'Is there a ghost in the machine?'

I feel rattled by the encounter. Who is he? Why was there a shock of light? What does the question mean?

I am just a regular Joe and my life is perfect.

* * *

The day continues in the usual manner. My colleague seems totally unfazed by this morning's interaction. Only I have been affected. I give Angela a call but she is too busy to chat. Poor woman is run off her feet working for a demanding and relentless boss. I leave a brief message saying how much I love her.

During my break I catch up with a couple of friends. It's just small talk and general chit-chat but it makes me feel better.

Scanning the news feed on my phone, an article jumps out at me. Titled 'The Candle Flame Is Blown Out', it interviews various psychologists and scientists about the Afterlife. The premise espoused by these eminent professionals is that when you die, it is similar to the extinguishing of a candle flame. You are gone. You cease to exist.

I lean back and stare at the ceiling. Never given the topic much thought. I believe in living in the here and now, fully immersing in the reality that surrounds me. Enjoying life as it presents itself. Celebrating what is. There is so much beauty right before us, why should we waste time worrying about the future? I shrug and raise my eyebrows. The article is pointless intellectual conjecture. Double-yawn.

I hear my name being called. Ah, the post-lunch rush. How will these overstressed souls make it until 6? I laugh softly. If the candle flame is indeed blown out, then what is this all for? Are we just a bunch of ants fighting over scraps of food and territory? Are we nothing more than the culmination of biological and psychological drives? Are we just sentient machines?

An hour later the queue subsides and I take a deep breath. Now it's me who needs a cappuccino. I sigh happily. One of the joyful perks of the job. I spend a few minutes creating an elaborate swirling vortex from chocolate syrup and foam. Seat myself near the door and sip leisurely. This is what life is about. Less thinking, less worrying, less surmising and speculating. It's about being. Fully present in every precious moment.

I have treasured my time with Angela. We married soon after meeting. Me 25, her 27. It's a good age. The turmoil of puberty and desperate quest for identity usually relent by the mid-20s. We wanted a family while still young and she became pregnant quickly. My dad used to say 'family is everything', that it creates solidarity, a rock upon which society is built. He pushed us to extend our commitment outward, to embrace our community and district. He called it the 'wider family'. I can still hear his words. 'Kindness, compassion and connection. Those are the important things.'

Rain pelting against the window. Snaps me out of my reverie. The coffee-house is empty. Time for clearing and cleaning. I am deeply grateful for my life. Built on sturdy values, established on principles of the heart, peace and joy were inevitable.

The Specials board has blown over. I hurry out to the sidewalk. Sudden gust of wind. A woman loses her umbrella and shouts in frustration. Rushing after it. The small dog is yapping noisily. Into the street. Reach out. Wind turns. Rain in my face. Can't see. WHUUMP!

Where did that umbrella go? Why are those people standing still? Mother covering her mouth, daughter pointing … what is it? … Aidan rushing out the coffee-house … lips moving … shouting … is he calling my name? … follow his eyes … someone lying in the road … awkward position … what happened? … Aidan kneeling over the body … dialling the phone … tears streaming … walk over … how terrible … place my hand on his shoulder … passes right through … what the … that face … incredible … no, wait, no … No! … it can't be …

Looking around … driver in expensive car … head in hands … I scream for help … no one notices … touch myself, I feel solid … a pedestrian strolls through me … what's going on? … "Aidan! Aidan!" … he doesn't hear me … paramedics arrive … ambulance … "Take care, that's my body!" … oh my … if I'm dead … Angela … Ryana … sweetheart … "Noooo!"

Stunned … stupefied … invisible in my world … cut off … watching events unfold … a mere spectator … powerless … helpless … my wife … my baby girl … who will look after them?

Police handcuffing the driver … bloodshot eyes … bespoke suit … people shaking their heads … the City takes another life … is he even sober?

They are pulling a sheet over my face ... oh my ... unable to deal with this ... this can't be happening ... my perfect life ... I turn and look at the coffee-house ... God, what now?

At the end of the street ... wide beam of light descending from the heavens ... peculiar and beautiful energy ... there's that dishevelled stranger ... walking just ahead ... rush after him ...

"Hey! Hey!"

He stops and turns.

"You can see me?"

Heartfelt gaze. Nod.

"Where are you going? What's happening to me?"

Points to the beam of light.

I catch up to him. Walk by his side.

Confused emotions. Tears. My world. My life. My family. Loss of everything I cherish. Peace. Stirrings of joy. Drawn toward the radiance. One existence finished. Strange thoughts and feelings.

"Am I going home?"

Gentle smile. Extends his hand.

I look up into the swirling vortex ... surreal ... exquisite ... ethereal ... celestial. Stare down the street one last time. I love you Angela and Ryana. I weep. I smile. I surrender.

Huge pulsating vortex with spiralling bright colours and millions of doors. Intensely loud scchhh! Completely disorienting.

Michael grabs my arm. *Pay attention. Most people miss this part.*

We surf along the energy stream until a glowing portal appears. The most beautiful Light is just ahead of us. We step through the door into a green-tinged world.

"Is this heaven?"

Really? Thought you were free of ideology.

"What happened to the Light?"

You are not ready for it. One step at a time.

"Is this another plane of existence?"

What do you think?

I shrug. "Whatever. I have nothing to chase or seek."

He smiles. *That's why I came to collect you.*

"Who usually shepherds human souls?"

Messengers. Sent to escort each point of consciousness during the transition.

"Transition to where?"

That depends on each being. What needs to be learned? What is sought?

"Why am I here?"

You chose here.

"I didn't know this place existed."

You don't choose with your mind. You choose with your energy. Your essence is drawn to where you belong. It's about the resonance of energies.

"Always?"

Sometimes you choose a challenging dimension in order to increase compassion, understanding or wisdom.

"The individual always chooses? Absolute free will?"

Every point of consciousness has a Guardian operating in its reality. A Messenger accompanies you when you transition between realities. These highly experienced and wise beings offer knowledge and guidance. Up to you to heed, adapt or ignore.

"You are obviously not a Guardian or Messenger. Who are you?"

A Keeper of the Light. Call me a maverick, if you prefer.

"Maverick?"

Unorthodox and independent-minded individual.

"Oh."

I am off to the sacred temple. Make yourself at home.

"Wait. What will I do here?"

I don't know. Free will, remember?

Why is he walking away from me? My reality has been completely shaken. Leaving me confused and disoriented and alone.

I watch transfixed as he shimmers into brilliance, soon burning so bright that it becomes impossible to look upon him.

Wow.

So that's a Keeper of the Light.

* * *

On my own. Endless landscape stretches before me. I float past the towering statues and into an expansive garden. Ethereal beings wander along stone pathways lined by dancing flowers. Sparkling translucent mists converse serenely near a lotus pond. I sit on a polished wooden bench under the embrace of a huge tree. A grand fountain sprays and babbles in the distance.

Two solitary weeks drift by. I do not leave the bench. Much to ponder.

Did I really choose this incredible place? Total immersion in peace, beauty and bliss? Why would a being choose any other destination?

A luminous hummingbird with green, silver and gold plumage alights on the armrest. Its tiny dark eyes seem to penetrate my core. I quickly feel uncomfortable and shoo it away.

It's hard to grieve under these conditions. I've never felt so happy. Hmm ... it's more than that ... the ambience ... a loving omniscient energy permeates the background ...

A feminine presence draws near.

Wassup?

"Excuse me?"

I have been assigned to you.

"You know who I am?"

Of course.

"What do I call you?"

How about M?

"M?"

Yeah. Short for messenger, mentor, mother –

"You don't have a real name?"

Are you referring to an Earth designation?

"Uh, I guess."

Soft whistle. Toto, we are not on Earth anymore.

"What does that mean?"

Really? You see my lips moving?

"I think so …"

You brought baggage.

"Huh?"

Conditioning clouds your perception.

The form shifts into a white-yellow sparkling ball of light.

"Wow."

Now into an ethereal white-yellow mist.

"Wait a minute. Do I look like you?"

Houston, we have a breakthrough.

It feels like my mind is tearing. Painful is an apt description. Jarring my head. Blurring my vision.

"Aaargghh!" I hear myself shouting.

Everything appears as vibrations against a backdrop of brilliant light. Multitudinous musical notes and spaces dancing on shimmering paper. One glorious extensive song sheet.

Ah, the doors of perception are cleansed.

"It's all pure energy, isn't it?"

Yep. Consciousness. Life. Light.

"I am pure consciousness."

Indeed. You've crossed the bridge.

"I can express in any form I choose?"

Everything is a thought-force. Think and be.

"So thought equals being?"

Thought is being. It's all consciousness.

"I am pure consciousness."

You want to start the lesson again?

"No."

Silence.

"It's confusing. Begs the question: Who am I?"

Welcome to the most fundamental question in your reality.

"I thought that was the 'ghost in the machine' query?"

That has been satisfactorily answered, has it not?

"Evidently."

Different reality, different question.

Wow. If I have a mind, it's reeling.

"I need some time alone."

Done.

Settled on the grass by the lotus pond, my eyelids nipping at each other. Yes, it's a manifestation of thought; it helps me understand my experience. Perhaps we don't sleep in this world but I yearn to disappear for a while. Is it possible to shut down and process this later? Everything fades into grey.

* * *

I wake up in the late morning. The shutters have been thrown open. A refreshing breeze dances across the duvet. The sun is shining brightly. I can see the ocean from my window. The glimmering waves with their frothy white peaks engender a wonderful calmness in me. Just perfect. What more could I want?

Wait a minute. This is not home. Am I creating this? Is this another manifestation of my thoughts?

Angela! Ryana! Where are they? How do I connect with them? I need to know how they are doing. Instantly I am standing before the lotus pond. A gentle ripple draws my attention. I gaze into the still water. There they are! How is this possible?

I watch them for an hour. Their grief is plain to see. Angela is not working. Both at home. Wish I could wrap my arms around them. Love them so much!

I know they cannot see or hear me. I reside in another dimension. No way to contact them.

Sadness rises within me. Then it spills from my being. Plunge to my knees, my body racked by sobs. A single tear falls from each eye, splashing softly onto the pond. At that moment Angela turns her head. "Joseph, is that you? We miss you, my darling! It hurts but we're coping."

Grief cascades over my being. I stare resolutely into the glassy water. Ryana looks up, giggles, waves. She cannot see me, surely. Does she sense my presence too? I wave back. "Daddy loves you, baby!" Another hour passes. The image gradually fades. What now? Do I have to let them go? Am I supposed to move on with my life? Will I ever see them again?

Eventually I drag myself to the polished wooden bench and gather my energy. Heave a big sigh. Love is a strange and precious thing. A life without love is not a life at all. It permeates your being and changes you. It is the most beautiful and fulfilling experience in the universe. It can never be taken away from you. The love you experience is yours forever.

The weeks and months pass. I visit the lotus pond often and connect with my loved ones. If a tear falls, they sense my presence. It's that simple. Of course, as time goes by, the burden of grief lessens and tears diminish. I guess that's the natural order of things. Everyone heals at their own pace. We move on in little stages. Only love remains.

I am slowly settling into my new home. This dimension is imbued and suffused with ineffable Love. It is difficult to hold onto grief, anger and sadness. And something else is happening to me. Hard to explain. It's like the rough edges of my identity and personality are being worn away. I was worried about losing my connection to Angela and Ryana; now I'm concerned that I may be losing myself. It makes no sense and feels rather surreal.

The question posed to the Messenger drifts across my mind: "Who am I?"

What was her response? *Welcome to the most fundamental question in your reality.*

Hmm … not a clue.

Stroll over to the grand fountain. Wade in the cool water. Repose under the serene sprays. Why not? Unsure who is creating this reality but I am going to enjoy every moment.

* * *

Many months have receded into the distance. A frown creases my forehead. I know that's not true. There is no time here. There are no markers, no beacons, no clocks. Apart from the ever-present Light and Love generating this blissful canvas, all reality is created by the beings who meander along the many paths.

The only sunrises and sunsets are the ones we imagine. The oceans, the mountains, the endless gardens, the trees, the flowers – all fabrications produced by beautiful thought. Yes, I love it here. Wherever here is.

Wassup!

Startled, I turn to face her.

"M! Haven't seen you for a while."

There are so many assumptions in that statement.

"Yeah, I know. You have no name. Time doesn't exist."

Indeed.

"Makes me wonder: Why bother speaking?"

Wow, you are making progress.

"Hey, I have a question."

Of course you do.

"I heard that some souls are greeted by their loved ones when they transition. You know, those who have previously left Earth."

Are you listening to yourself?

"What do you mean?"

Ass-umptions.

"You don't seem very spiritual."

Check your baggage.

Uncomfortable silence. Wish I was back at the coffee-house. Life was simpler.

This being reminds me of someone. A long, long time ago. She used to dance with wild abandon. Sing at the top of her voice. Creative, unconventional, aberrant. Didn't take anything too seriously. There were always flowers in the house. Paintings. The memory hurts.

Staring at the ethereal glowing mist.

Oh! Could it be?

Welcome home, son.

I burst into tears. "Mom – is that – really – you?"

An aspect of me was your mother.

She pulls me into a close embrace.

"I have missed you!"

I love you, son.

"Why did you leave? I was so young."

Life happens. We can't control everything.

"Why didn't you say earlier?"

Each being is greeted by their own ideology and beliefs. A religious person perceives an angel or religious figure. Spiritual people with limited perspectives apply their own labels. Atheists often struggle in the beginning. In truth, a Messenger is just a messenger.

"Loved ones never greet transitioning souls?"

Of course they do.

"Oh."

However, consider the most fundamental question in your reality.

"Not that again."

You'll understand when you are ready.

"Who am I?"

Exactly.

"I have been here a while. Every day another scale falls from my eyes."

You and every being in this dimension.

"Every day I see a little clearer."

Uh huh. The doors of perception.

"I thought I was free of ideology."

She bursts into raucous laughter.

What if you are not you?

"Huh?"

Let's sit down by the fireplace. Pull up a chair.

I look around. "What fireplace?"

She smiles. *This one.*

And just like that, we are home. Mommy and me. The kitchen is warm. Kettle is boiling. Shrill whistle. My long socks keep my feet warm. Wrapping my hands around the mug of cocoa. What a treat!

She ruffles my hair. *Biscuits?*

"Yes, please!"

I am a teenager. Gruff with mother. Shrugging off affection. Swirling across the ice. As a goalie, must defend my team. No puck crosses this line. Zero score. Shootout. It's on me. Successful block. Thrilling feeling. Team scores. We're the champions!

I walk into the coffee-house. Love the aroma and hubbub. It's where I am meant to be. Growing into the role. What is a barista? I shrug. Just a title. It's about doing what I love. Nothing more, nothing less. Carving out designs with chocolate syrup and foam. Elated smiles. Satisfied customers.

She is walking down the aisle. I am trembling slightly, holding back the tears. Instructed not to cry lest I make her cry and ruin her make-up. Heart fluttering. Emotions all over the place. Cameras whirring. Pledge of vows. Passionate kiss. Jubilation. Celebration. Party all night.

Angela splayed in the birthing pool, exhausted after hours of labour. I am weeping. Feel so helpless. My wife looks like she has run a marathon. There is nothing I can do but offer kind words of encouragement. The midwife struggles. Breakthrough. Angela lying on mauve cushions. Soggy baby reclining on her chest. How can one describe that demeanour? Fatigue, bliss, love, all rolled into one. The three of us cuddle. Midwife takes a photo. Snip. Crying. New life begins.

At home, washing the dishes. She slips her arms around me and looks at me in that magical way. Ryana trundles toward us. I hoist her in the air with an ebullient "I love you!"

WHUUMP!

Find myself in a green-tinged world. Shocked and emotional.

Lengthy quietude. Stillness. Reflection.

My beautiful son, who is the real you? The child, the teenager, the adult, the husband, the father?

I blink slowly. Oh, I see.

"My identity changed many times. My knowledge and experience increased. However, I am neither my identity nor my knowledge. The real me sits behind it all, watching and witnessing."

Affectionate smile. *Excellent answer.*

Frowning. Massaging my temples thoughtfully.

It's like an actor immersing himself in a film or television role. The deeper into the character he goes, the more he learns and experiences. During his career he plays many characters. Each role affects him, changes him. Each character expands his awareness. The deeply immersed actor is in fact a conglomerate of all his roles. The wise actor remains a witness.

My hands make a T-sign.

Time out?

"Yep. I need to process that last one."

It's a natural progression. You're on the path.

I embrace her tightly. "Don't go too far."

Eyes sparkle kindness. *Think of me and I'll be here.*

I desperately need an ocean. Check. Tall palm trees swaying in a cool breeze. Check. Swooshing sound to soothe my fatigued consciousness. Check. Hmm … pink-and-gold sky. Check. Ah, hammock for the finishing touch.

I take a deep breath and sigh. The hammock swings gently. It is not long before I drift into a contented slumber.

* * *

Yawn and huge stretch. I have to smile. Old habits linger. There is no physical body to stretch. And I don't require sleep. It seems I still borrow thoughts and behaviour from my time on Earth. Perhaps it is a coping mechanism while I assimilate higher truths and adapt to this new existence.

Imagine a world of almost no limitations. You want to levitate? Do it. Surf the star-lit heavens? What are you waiting for? Appear as your favourite musician? Why not? The curious thing is, you are so filled with love and bliss in this dimension that those games soon lose their appeal.

No one is watching your childlike exploits. No one notices your inane costume-changes. Every being here is too fulfilled to be drawn into frivolous distractions. It's kind of refreshing. You have no choice but to truly embrace yourself. Do what you love. Connect with beings who resonate with you. It encourages a deeply honest existence.

At the same time, nobody is judging you. You are free to do what you want. Most importantly, you are free to express your being in its current resonance. In this moment, a meditation by the serene lake ... now, a glorious painting across the sky ... now, a heartfelt conversation with an advanced soul ... now, a wild dance across a sun-kissed meadow.

It seems an unspoken code is scrawled upon the backdrop of this world.

Every step is on the path.

"Aah!"

You ok?

"Do you have to sneak up like that?"

Was I sneaking?

"Next time wave a flag or something."

What about trumpets?

"Perhaps a gentle flute."

Noted.

"Wassup?"

Hint of a smile. *You were thinking of the unspoken code.*

"Yes."

Every step is on the path.

"Oh, now you've ruined it."

I have?

"Unspoken, remember?"

You're settling in nicely.

Deep-blue clouds rolling overhead. Gorgeous luminous raindrops begin spattering the trees and flowers. Daffodils are glistening. Serenity blankets us.

"It's quite beautiful. Is that you?"

No.

"It's me, isn't it?"

Uh huh.

"Is this another transition?"

Yep.

"Am I going somewhere?"

Who are you?

A tear escapes my eye and streams down my face.

"I'm not Joseph, am I?"

Delicate hand on my shoulder.

"Joseph is one aspect of me. I am waking up. I have been many beings."

You have indeed.

"Joseph is not dying. He is simply integrating into the entire me."

Is it uncomfortable?

I shake my head. "No. Just strange."

Stillness cascades along the countryside.

"Wow. I have been alive a long, long time."

Gentle smile.

"I remember now. Was I asleep? Lost in a vivid dream?"

In a sense.

"Go on. I know you want to say it."

Welcome home.

"Any advice?"

Just be with it.

"Every step is on the path?"

Indeed.

I stroll along the embankment and lay on the soft grass. The rain sinks into me, through me, watering the thirsty soil, feeding the hungry earth. The daffodils penetrate my hands and legs. A lotus flower emerges from my belly. I am part of this entire fabric of existence. I giggle quietly, close my eyes and surrender.

* * *

I understand now that every being undergoes this transition. No one pushes you. Everything flows naturally, in accordance with your state of mind, your readiness, the evolution of your consciousness. The Messengers primarily guide and support the process.

My most recent life has dissolved into my essence. To state it more correctly, I have absorbed and assimilated the experiences of Joseph. That life has merged with all my other lives. With everyone and everything I have ever been. Sure, Joseph was unconsciously influenced by the previous lives but, for the most part, he lived fresh and new. And this is how it is. How can an actor immerse in a new character if he still holds the previous characters within himself? You have to compartmentalise, you have to forget, to truly live a new life.

Residing in one's higher consciousness tends to reveal interesting truths. As Joseph, I was expressed in human form on Earth. I now recall wild adventures as a cheetah, an eagle and a dolphin. Even more interesting – I have not spent all my lifetimes on Earth. There are many planets and dimensions that I have inhabited. Numerous beings, countless stories.

When I arrived on Earth my previous lives were suppressed into my deepest unconscious. This facilitated a new beginning. The opportunity to see reality with untainted eyes, to open to innovative lessons and ideas. To love someone unknown and unfamiliar. To build exotic dreams.

I surmise that some beings regret that choice. Perhaps they are haunted by vague memories of exquisite dimensions and beautiful planets, of a different way of life, of deep love, of euphoric freedom and glorious flight. The subtle hints that swirl deep within the mind possibly engender frustration and depression. However, there is a reason they chose to forget.

It reminds me of a story. One thousand people trapped in a huge blacked-out warehouse. No visible doors or windows. Everyone scrambling to find the light switch. Once in a while a sliver of light appears and someone shouts "I've found it! I have the answer." People rush over to a corner and eagerly digest the sliver of light. Some become disciples, developing rock-solid beliefs, inflexible ideologies and intricate rituals. Others keep seeking. A month later, someone discovers another sliver of light. A few people integrate the knowledge and advance their thinking. Others convert to the new way. Conflict occurs between disciples of different factions, each adamant they know what's beyond the darkness. And so it continues.

The true seekers say "That's interesting." They acknowledge the various smidgens of illumination but ignore the temptation to root into a particular belief. A few beings quit believing in anything. One or two sit alone in the darkness.

Ah, the sound of a gentle flute.

That's some heavy surmising.

"Yeah, I guess it is."

You think Earth is a blacked-out room?

"Sure felt like it. No one really knew anything."

What about all the religious teachings?

"Mmm … slivers of light."

And new-age spirituality?

"Often just as limited."

There's no way out?

"Guardians and Messengers?"

Guardians are bound to a particular reality, such as Earth, for the duration of their assignments. Messengers can move freely between various realities.

"What is their function outside this dimension?"

Teachers and guides. Bound to the Three Immutable Laws.

"Remind me again?"

You may not reveal yourself. You may not interfere with free will. You may not interrupt the flow of Life.

"How can they guide humans without breaking the laws?"

You sense their presence, yet they do not reveal themselves. They flow encouragement into your energy field, yet they do not interfere. They whisper beneficial hints, yet they do not interrupt the flow of Life.

"Hmm. That doesn't alleviate human frustration."

All consciousness must develop at its own pace. Hence, the policy of non-interference. Besides, you cannot move a being's awareness forward by coercion, intimidation or shock. It is always contingent on the soul's current state of evolution and readiness.

"Hints, whispers and subtle pointers."

Exactly.

"In the dark room, impatience and frustration are balanced by readiness and evolution."

Consider your progress in this dimension. Your awareness expands only when you can handle it. You are supported by an ambience of love and freedom, and the occasional prompt, but the veils only drop when you are ready.

"Touché."

As for the dark room ...

"Yes?"

You left out the person who discovers the inner door and transcends that reality.

"So there is a way out."

Actually it's a way in.

"What do you mean?"

Seeking outward is not the answer. No exit strategy is required.

"Hmm. An entrance strategy?"

Why chase slivers of light? The Light you seek is inside you.

"Aha."

The door is located within each point of consciousness.

"It was there all along?"

Behind that door is the Light that every being seeks.

"Who can show us the door? Guardians? Messengers?"

Those who have already walked through the door. The enlightened ones.

"How can we identify them?"

They exude a radiant Light. They walk in deep peace, joy and bliss.

"Are they all teachers and guides?"

Recluses. Painters. Carpenters. Aeroplane mechanics. Philanthropists. Writers. Teachers.

"What about the teachings?"

Words are just seeds. The Light is the answer.

"Are there many enlightened ones?"

A handful in each reality.

"Why so few?"

They don't have to manifest anymore.

"Why do they stay?"

Those who remain made a choice.

"What choice?"

Love.

"Oh."

Quietude is a drop creating ripples in my mind.

"Wow, this got pretty deep."

She leaps into the air, grabs a luscious fruit from an overhanging mauve tree, shouts *Whoo hoo!* then falls to the ground and rolls about with laughter.

I gaze at the quirky Messenger.

"Let's go for a swim. Shake these notions. Clear my head."

Know any good oceans?

"Coming right up ..."

The rigid physical aspects of Earth simplified life and reality. I exist. You exist. Things exist. My body walks and moves. Your body walks and moves. We think. We talk. We interact.

Now we are swimming in waves that I have created. In fact, the waves are me. And I am the waves. My sleek body flows smoothly over the white tips, every ebb and flow a projection of my thoughts.

I am apprehensive about fully embracing my true nature. It seems I am nothing but thought. At some point I won't need these projections and manifestations. I will simply allow myself to *be* thought. But that time is not here yet.

I dive deep into the crystal clear water. A school of fish shimmer and dance around me. It feels wonderfully natural and comforting. Two large dolphins cavorting beneath the powerful waves. A sense of freedom pervades my being.

Later we make our way to shore. Collapsing on a glistening white beach, I stare up at the brilliant sun. What has happened to me? Too much thinking, surmising and speculating. It's supposed to be about being. Fully present in every precious moment.

I used to be a regular Joe and my life was perfect. I close my eyes and drift into the swoosh of the ocean waves. Tomorrow is another day. Oh yeah, no time. Whatever.

* * *

How do I describe the passing of time when there is no measuring device? Perhaps the equivalent of a year has elapsed.

On Earth I paid no attention to the musings of spiritual people. I ignored religion, labelling it as the 'blind leading the blind'. I preferred to live in the here and now, celebrating life as it presented itself, learning to enjoy every moment, filling my mind with gratitude.

I heard people talk about heaven, life after death and The Other Side. But it was all speculation, beliefs and theories. Truth is, no one knew. No one could honestly say what happens when the physical body dies. Every human carries a fear of death. It's never acknowledged; it's not discussed openly; it doesn't appear in the news feeds. It's buried beneath our everyday lives.

It's that fear and apprehension that cause us to speculate and believe. For some of us, a desperate hope is instilled. We must live beyond physical death. Life must go on. The thought of being a mere candle flame blown out is untenable. We cling to religious and spiritual myths to allay that unbearable possibility.

The fact is, each one of us will undergo the change. We will leave our physical bodies, young or old, sick or healthy. We will lose everything we treasure. We will transition to the next dimension. There is absolutely nothing you can take with you. Except knowledge, memories and love. Those are yours to keep forever. Those become part of your essence.

The transition occurs in stages. It largely depends on where you are at spiritually. It depends on the choices you made, the attitudes you hold, the beliefs you cradle.

It's all a journey. Whether you jump from Earth to this glorious dimension, whether you spend dozens of lifetimes on Earth, whether you move between planets and ethereal worlds, it's still a journey. And you are at the centre. You are the helmsman. You choose, you steer, you travel. It's completely in your hands.

There is no destination. It is not about accomplishing anything. It is truly about being. Being you. Expressing your beautiful and radiant essence. Learning not to indulge fear, rather to embrace love. Love for who you are. Love for other beings. Love toward all that exists. Love toward Existence itself.

The journey is a natural progression. One of the greatest secrets is surrender. Openness. Freedom and flexibility. To ask these questions: What is possible? What can be? What limitations beset my thinking? What beliefs cloister my being? Why follow this path? Why not?

The mind yearns to be free. The spirit wishes to soar. The veils of perception need to drop and disappear. It turns out that we are all connected. That we live forever. That we are unending consciousness. Right now, this is your reality. There is nothing to do, nowhere to go, nothing to seek or chase. This is your life, your world, your joy and bliss. Laying right before you. Like a book just waiting to be read. Dust off the cover, open to page one and fall into yourself.

There is nothing to do but live your life. Live it to the best of your ability. Choose to be happy. Open your mind. Fling the gates of your heart wide open. Run through a meadow, smell the flowers, touch the rain. Invite the stars to shower your being. Do a random kindness for a stranger. Surf into the possibilities that life offers. Take chances. Express your feelings. Share your thoughts. Connect. Sing. Dance. Love.

Wow, you've come a long way.

"Michael!" I have this strange urge to bow.

What happened to Joseph?

"Absorbed into my essence."

Got any plans?

Ironic. After my lengthy musing.

"Celebrating what is."

Some things never change.

"Yeah, I guess."

There's someone I'd like you to meet.

A luminous hummingbird with green, silver and gold plumage hovers around my head. Tiny dark eyes staring at me. I curb the impulse to swat it away.

An interesting point of consciousness.

Indeed.

No desire to seek or chase.

A master of being.

Penetrating gaze counters my silence.

Makes a delicious cappuccino too.

A fondness and disposition for physical worlds.

Surfed the high winds as an eagle, relaxed in the ocean currents as a dolphin, soaked up the African sun as a cheetah.

"I'm right here, you know."

Many names, many lives.

Greetings, Lao Tzu.

"That was a long time ago."

6th century BC, Earth time.

"I know. I was there."

Michael laughs softly.

Still the Old Sage.

Befitting designation.

"I thought we didn't use names here."

Casual shrug. 'Michael' is useful sometimes.

"Call me Old Sage. I don't care."

The hummingbird flutters around me then settles on a nearby branch. A fabulous sunrise glimmers over the distant horizon, soft rays peeping across the trees. A flurry of blue and green butterflies streams along the grassland. Brightly coloured flowers turn their heads and salute the shimmering orb. Wordless and entranced, we watch the magnificent spectacle.

Impressive. Captivating.

"Wu wei."

Non-action. Doing without doing.

I smile. "Harmony with the Tao."

Was it pronounced Tao or Dao?

"Tao."

Now there's a mystery.

"Hence, the Tao Te Ching."

May as well be quantum physics.

I burst into laughter.

"Tao Te Ching means The Way of Virtue and Power. As I wrote in the first lines: 'The Tao that can be told is not the eternal Tao. The name that can be named is not the eternal name.'"

Beyond unfathomable.

"A Keeper of the Light understands its unutterable nature."

Indeed.

"Search your heart and see, the way to do is to be."

Michael bows deferentially before me.

I am taken aback. "Not necessary."

Greetings, Dōgen Zenji.

"What is this? Are we going through all my lives?"

It's called a review for a reason.

"Oh."

1200 - 1253, Earth time.

"Again, I know. I was there."

Michael caresses the pink and white blossoms of a Japanese Cherry. Then his gaze falls upon the glistening ground.

I can't resist. "The whole moon and entire sky are reflected in one dewdrop on the grass."

Contemplative smile.

"Are we finished the review now?"

Why the resistance?

"Genjōkōan means Actualising the Fundamental Point. As I wrote in that essay: 'To study the Way is to study the Self. To study the Self is to forget the self. To forget the self is to be enlightened by all things of the universe.'"

You've forgotten the self?

"Ancient wisdom."

I glance at the luminous hummingbird.

Greetings, Dajian Huineng.

"Really?"

638 - 713, Earth time.

"We're going backward now?"

Does time exist?

"Let me remind you of an event. In that life, I sought out Hongren the Fifth Patriarch at his monastery on Huang Mei Mountain. Overcoming his disdain for my heritage, I became a labourer in the monastery. One day Hongren announced a contest to find his successor: 'Write a poem to explain the Essence of Mind.'

"Shenxiu wrote this poem: 'The body is a Bodhi tree, The mind a mirror bright, At all times polish it diligently, And let no dust alight.'

"There were no other challengers, so I stepped up and recited as follows: 'The body is no Bodhi tree, The mind no mirror bright, Since nothing at the root exists, On what should dust alight?'

"As you know, I became the Sixth Patriarch."

And what did you teach?

"I favoured the Diamond Sutra."

The Vajracchedikā Prajñāpāramitā Sūtra?

"That's the one. Translation?"

Diamond Cutter Perfection Of Wisdom.

"Precisely."

And where did that originate?

I smile wryly. "Lao Tzu."

Ah, the mystery of it all.

"Transcribed in the presence of Siddhartha."

Gautama Buddha?

"Of course."

And the teaching elucidates?

"All forms, thoughts and concepts are illusory. Surrender your limited notions of reality. The way is neither through the mind nor the body. Give up the self. Live without attachment. Cultivate without attainment."

I am noticing a thread.

"Beyond the Tao everything is a dream, a phantom, a drop of dew, a flash of lightning. Observe, approach, interact, meditate in this fashion: Reality is transient and impermanent."

The Tao Te Ching states: 'The Tao is both named and nameless. As nameless it is the origin of all things; as named it is the Mother of 10,000 things.'

"Indeed."

Profound silence cloaks us. Tiny dark eyes bore into my essence.

Watching ... waiting ...

"Aaargghh!" I grab my temples.

You ok?

"The Tao is everything, everywhere, everywhen. It is the birth-cry of the universe. It is the death of the universe. It is the breath of the universe. The Tao is timeless. The Tao Is."

Does it hurt?

I smile. "Not at all."

Welcome to the next level.

The hummingbird tilts its head as if assessing me. Then it fires up its wings and disappears.

"What was that all about?"

Every being is subjected to a review.

"After transitioning realities?"

Of course.

"Why?"

To determine where you've been and what you've learned.

"Why do you need to know?"

It's not for us, Old Sage.

"For whom?"

The helmsman. The captain of the ship.

"Who exactly is that?"

You.

* * *

I am sitting on the polished wooden bench near the fountain. It is a strange situation. Death of a human body, death of a character, death of an identity. Kind of bizarre. It's incredible how we tend to hold onto possessions and beliefs when we are immersed in the theatre of a particular reality. Earth certainly has that seductive quality.

Imagine the shock an atheist may experience when relocating to a new dimension. And the avaricious stockbroker, the greedy banker, the self-absorbed narcissist, the fame-hungry celebrity. I burst into laughter at the thought.

Is that a flute?

Hey.

"Hey."

How's everything going?

"I don't know. It seems alone time is hard to find."

You wish to be alone?

"Just trying to catch up with all my thoughts."

Still thinking …

"Yep. What would I be without my thoughts?"

One of the most fundamental questions –

"Enough with the fundamental questions. Yes, there is a ghost in the machine. Yes, I have remembered who I am."

You think that question is resolved?

"Which one?"

The moment you left your human body and transposed to a new reality, it became evident that you are more than a biological machine. The second question, however, is more enduring.

"It is?"

Uh huh.

"The veils of perception have dropped. I recall all my lifetimes. Every identity. I know that I am not the eagle, the dolphin, the cheetah. I am not Joseph or Lao Tzu or Huineng. Those were characters I was playing. I am beyond those beings. I am ..."

Yes?

"Um ..."

Who am I, if not those characters?

"Uh ..."

Aha.

"I am a point of consciousness."

Mmm.

"I am a point of consciousness. I think. I create. I experience."

Ok.

"And I feel a bit lonely."

You were complaining about not enough alone time.

"I like my own company ... these transitions require much assimilation ... I miss Angela and Ryana but they were connected to one aspect of me ..." The forlorn sigh surprises me. "I don't know what I want."

Thing is, once you shed all the characters and revert to pure consciousness, it can feel a bit lonely. Every being wants to connect to other beings. To converse, share, reciprocate.

"Yeah ... the occasional discussion is not enough."

Long pause. Finally, a serious countenance. *Do you plan on returning to Earth? Are there other dimensions calling you?*

"No. This is the most beautiful place I have ever been. The love and peace exuding from this reality are extraordinary. I just need more ... connection ... belonging ..."

I guess you are ready.

"Ready for what?"

The knowledge bank.

"Huh?"

Once we plug your consciousness into the knowledge bank, everything changes. You have to be certain about this transition though.

"Another transition? You sneaky monkey."

Remind me: Who's in control of your life?

"Uh, me." I gaze at my toes. Then laughter grips me. I have no toes. When will I give up these antiquated projections?

All beings in this dimension are constantly uploading their knowledge and experiences into a boundless repository. Once connected, you will automatically be uploading your knowledge too. This naturally correlates with a dissolution of privacy.

"What about personal boundaries?"

They quickly vanish.

"And private thoughts?"

Everything is shared openly. Privacy is redundant.

"Wow."

You haven't asked about the upside.

"What's the upside?"

Universal connection. A sublime sense of belonging. Instant and open communication. Access to the immense knowledge bank.

"Impressive."

Essentially you are tapping into the collective consciousness of innumerable beings. Imagine that vast amount of knowledge made available to you.

"What about free will?"

Once you are plugged in, we assume full control of your mind. We effectively own you.

"Seriously?"

Ebullient laughter. Of course not! Free will is one of our most valued tenets.

"No private thoughts ..."

Everything is known and shared.

"You cannot even lie?"

The collective consciousness means we operate with transparency, openness and honesty. There is nothing to hide and no need for deceit. There is also no loneliness. We enjoy a natural form of empathy. It's called love.

"That's what I miss most of all."

She unrolls a lengthy faded parchment.

Excellent. Just sign here ... and here.

"Stop teasing me."

It's a big step.

"Yeah ..."

Almost forgot ...

"What?"

No more gentle flutes.

"Meaning?"

The flipside of never being lonely is never being alone.

"That's a lot to consider."

Indeed. You want to be alone now?

"I do ..."

A long walk through the expansive gardens. Still have mixed feelings. I enjoy the solitude, the quietude. Admiring the exquisite roses and carnations along the way. Just ahead a huge African Baobab tree. I sprawl in the magnificent sunshine, catching the last of the summer rays. A sapphire ocean beckons me. Sleek silver body exploring the serene depths. Break the surface. Large wings spreading, feathery tips searching for a thermal. Soar into the stratosphere. Lao Tzu, bowing, meditation, teaching, writing, Huineng, insight, wisdom. Characters flashing past me, dipping in, dipping out, Earth, other planets, dimensions, body forms, languages, cultures, civilizations, whirring, whirring, whirring.

"Enough!" I shout. "Enough."

Reflective pause. Weary sigh.

"I've had enough."

Strange energy approaching. At once apprehensive; yet filled with delightful anticipation. This is in my hands. Only my consent is required.

A few moments gazing at a radiant Peruvian lily, a tall plant blooming in gorgeous shades of purple, yellow and orange. I take a deep breath. Nod solemnly.

A single tear falls from my eye. Once again, I am saying goodbye to all I know. Crossing the next bridge. Leaping into the unknown.

* * *

Falling. Falling. Falling. Deep purple swirling. Blackness. Nothing.

Switch.

Overwhelming sound. Millions of whispers. Cascades of light. Clutching my head.

"Help me!"

It's ok. I'm right here.

"Too much information ..."

You'll get used to it. Try to focus.

"Focus?"

Your intention controls the flow.

"So much light."

All light, all consciousness.

"Stop."

Unsteady sensation. Peace settles.

That's it. Hold a clear intention.

Frowning. "Myriad information … intention dictates direction …"

As always.

"Oh!"

Mmm …?

"Wowwwww!"

My entire being feels … loved … no longer an ambient sensation … it is inside me! Streams of love and peace flowing through me … I am in the surging river … everything connected …

If I had eyes, tears would be gushing … phenomenal … breathtaking … extraordinary …

I am viewing a spectacular mountain range brushed by two full moons … softly tweeting birds … swoosh of a nearby ocean … scent of jasmine … whose experience is this?

All our experiences are shared. Information, knowledge, feelings, memories. Full immersion.

"Never imagined ... how wonderful ..."

Disappearing into astounding scenery ... awe-inspiring landscapes ... astonishing worlds ... like walking into a favourite film and staying there ... only these films are new and yet to be navigated ...

Long while later, I am reminded of her presence.

If you need me, just call.

"Intention?"

The key that fits all locks.

"Thank you."

I will leave you now.

"In a manner of speaking."

Kind smile.

Indeed.

* * *

You could spend lifetimes surfing the knowledge bank. It's a limited descriptor for such a profound ... experience. Far more than merely offering vast amounts of data, it embraces the entire being and permeates the consciousness with connection, compassion and belonging.

It's beyond beautiful. In this magnificent house are many mansions. Innumerable doorways. Boundless rooms. And every one is home.

And the price tag? The surrender of the tiresome self.

I wonder how many people on Earth (and other planets) are weary of maintaining an identity, a persona, an image. The constant projection. The relentless pretence among other actors, all clueless or in denial about their real selves.

Deep in our hearts we know those projections are flimsy fabrications. Beings furthest from the Truth are usually the most entrenched in a particular identity, ideology or belief system. It's like standing in cement and pretending to be happy.

You are pure consciousness having an experience in a limited reality. You are not your persona, image or identity. That belongs to the character you play in a peculiar and captivating theatre. True joy comes from understanding and embracing your limitless nature.

Every day you face a blank canvas. A bubble of infinite possibility. What will you choose? Is your mind allowed to roam free? Can you surrender into your deepest being? Can you flow among the wild and wonderful experiences that present themselves to you? Will you remember that you are a creator?

Live your life here and now. Breathe. Laugh. Dance. Celebrate. And when you are ready, a bridge will appear, beckoning you to the next level. Life is a series of transitions. No need to seek them. They are seeking you.

Leave you alone for a moment.

I laugh softly.

The king of contemplation.

"There's a lot to reflect upon."

Slow nod.

"Vast knowledge unattached to ego."

No one infringes upon your viewpoint.

"Freedom to think, dream, ponder."

Conversations when requested.

"No advice."

Perhaps the occasional hint.

"Pure loving connection."

A large blue butterfly flaps gently overhead. Stardust scatters in its wake. Ruby and coral tulips sway in the light breeze. Scent of strawberries and vanilla teases my taste buds. Divine mauve fruit reveals its secret seeds. Subtle symphony of sonorous bliss.

"Spectacular. Where is that?"

The dimension before this one.

"Oh."

Hmm.

"How do you travel there?"

She looks at me strangely.

Uh oh.

Quietness pervades the dream.

Frantically search my thoughts.

"You are going to tell me there is no space."

A dimension is not a place. You are not travelling through distance when you transition.

"Aha. What is a dimension?"

Dimensions are expressions of Life. As you shift your consciousness, you can step into various dimensions.

"We are currently operating in one dimension."

Are we?

I shake my head. "Whoa. Slow down. I've only just transitioned. One dimension, myriad voices, vast knowledge, countless experiences."

Yep.

"Is this heaven?"

A grain of truth in your ideology.

"Meaning?"

This dimension is very close to the Source.

"The Source?"

Access the knowledge bank.

It takes only a moment.

"The underlying Is-ness, Tao, Light."

Indeed.

"We journey toward the Source."

Do you remember your transition from Earth?

"Uh huh."

Huge pulsating vortex with spiralling bright colours and millions of doors?

"We move along those doors, travelling toward the Source."

Only there is no distance, no space.

"Space is an illusion?"

Dimensions are not places. They are expressions of Life.

Take a deep breath. Amble to the Baobab tree. Sit on a bench hewn from rock. Blazing sun soaking into my skin. I can work this out. The understanding is near.

Pick up a handful of flat pebbles. Cast them at the lake ... bouncing and skipping across the azure water ... watching the ever-expanding ripples ...

Oh.

I heave a sigh.

"It's not really a journey, is it?"

No.

"I'm standing still."

You are neither still nor moving.

"Just being."

You are a point of consciousness having an experience.

"Immersed in a film?"

A deeply layered film.

"I see what I am ready to see."

Exactly. The veils of perception.

"When my awareness expands, a veil drops."

That's the transition.

"Aha."

Stroke my chin thoughtfully.

"I am not going anywhere. No distance is traversed. The transition is simply the opening and expanding of my awareness."

And the dimensions?

"They are not places but points of awareness."

No journey. Just expanding awareness.

"The vortex ... the Light at the end ... the doors ..."

Perceptual points. Hence, the doors of perception.

Oh my ... it all makes sense now.

"As the doors of perception are cleansed ... as my awareness expands ... I move through dimensions ... eventually reaching the Light."

Every point of consciousness journeys toward the Light.

"Why?"

She stands up and shimmers.

That's enough for one day. Haven't you some musing to do?

I stare at the sparkling white-yellow mist.

"What are you waiting for?"

Hesitancy lingers in the air.

"Welcome to the next level?"

Resolute gaze.

Ah.

"Welcome to the next perceptual point?"

That's the one.

I am alone with my thoughts. Oh yeah. The entire conversation has been uploaded to the knowledge bank. Perhaps it will help shift another being's awareness.

I fling my arms into the sky and become the soaring eagle. A brilliant sun lies just ahead.

Breathing the rarefied air.

Marvelling at the new insight. Imagine …

It's not a journey but the dropping of the veils of perception.

* * *

A new day dawns. Soft sunrays glimmer across the horizon.

I have decided to take a year off. How else can I describe it?

So many transitions … awareness expansions … perceptual shifts.

I need to digest it all. Slow down. Meditate.

Considering that I can create any reality, I have chosen to replicate Lake Manasarovar on Mount Kailash, Tibet, Earth. Interestingly, Lake Manasarovar means Lake of Consciousness or Lake of Mind.

I am laying on a yellow cashmere blanket, breathing the thin crisp air, staring at a radiant blue sky. Incredibly beautiful. Comforting.

Reposing in the tranquil ripples of reflective reminiscence.

My life as a barista … delicious cappuccinos … gorgeous coffee art.

A short walk down a tree-lined avenue to our small apartment.

The pitter-patter of little feet. "Daddy? Daddy?" The second love of my life. Sweeping my gorgeous two-year-old into my arms and holding her tight.

Kissing Angela. Evening cuddles and enjoyable conversations.

A man with unkempt long dark hair, olive skin, unshaven.

Shock of light.

The most fundamental question in your reality.

Scrawled across the immaculate white napkin in fine cocoa powder, the words: 'Is there a ghost in the machine?'

I hurry out to the sidewalk. Sudden gust of wind. A woman loses her umbrella and shouts in frustration. Rushing after it. Rain in my face. WHUUMP!

Huge pulsating vortex with spiralling bright colours and millions of doors.

First transition.

Keeper of the Light. Guardians. Messengers.

Wassup?

Everything is energy and consciousness.

"Begs the question: Who am I?"

The most fundamental question in your reality.

Connecting to my family at the lotus pond.

The limitation of ideology and beliefs.

The illusion of identity.

It's like an actor immersing himself in a film or television role.

The life of Joseph integrating into my essence.

Remembering and assimilating numerous lifetimes.

Luminous hummingbird with green, silver and gold plumage hovering around my head. Tiny dark eyes staring at me.

Every being is subjected to a review.

"After transitioning realities?"

Of course.

"Why?"

To determine where you've been and what you've learned.

"Why do you need to know?"

It's not for us, Old Sage.

"For whom?"

The helmsman. The captain of the ship.

"Who exactly is that?"

You.

Introduction to the knowledge bank.

All beings in this dimension are constantly uploading their knowledge and experiences into a boundless repository. Once connected, you will automatically be uploading your knowledge too. This naturally correlates with a dissolution of privacy.

"What about personal boundaries?"

They quickly vanish.

"And private thoughts?"

Everything is shared openly. Privacy is redundant.

"Wow."

You haven't asked about the upside.

"What's the upside?"

Universal connection. A sublime sense of belonging. Instant and open communication. Access to the immense knowledge bank.

"Impressive."

The collective consciousness means we operate with transparency, openness and honesty. There is nothing to hide and no need for deceit. There is also no loneliness. We enjoy a natural form of empathy. It's called love.

Connected. Overwhelming whispers. Vast knowledge. Belonging. Love.

"Intention?"

The key that fits all locks.

"We move along those doors, travelling toward the Source."

Dimensions are not places. They are expressions of Life.

No journey. Just expanding awareness.

"The vortex ... the Light at the end ... the doors ..."

Perceptual points. Hence, the doors of perception.

"As the doors of perception are cleansed ... as my awareness expands ... I move through dimensions ... eventually reaching the Light."

Catching the upward current and soaring into the stratosphere.

Marvelling at the new insight. Imagine ...

It's not a journey but the dropping of the veils of perception.

* * *

I have decided to grow a beard. A long white one. The azure robe and gnarled wooden staff probably make me appear as a wizard.

The only limitation to form is the imagination. It seems that intention is everything. Intention is the rudder of the ship. The switch in the railway line. The stone that diverts the stream.

It is strange how my consciousness can manifest in virtually unlimited ways. If I think of a particular being, there she is. If I dream of a place, it appears. I understand that I am creating this reality but it still amazes me.

The instantaneous connection with countless beings is breathtaking. There is seldom a question that cannot be answered, either by downloading information from the knowledge bank or by discourse with wise entities.

The idea that I am unmoving, that there is no journey, that everything is an experience of my consciousness ... well, that's unsettling ... confusing ...

Nothing actually moves. Everything is simply a flash of thought, diluted by one's perceptual filters. If there is any kind of journey, it is a journey of consciousness. It's like sitting in a cinema watching a variety of films. You are not going anywhere.

There is just the watcher and that which is watched. But that which is watched is dependent on the perceptual filters, on the current state of awareness.

I am not only the watcher but I am also creating that which I watch. I am the watcher and the watched!

Seriously?

"M"

I thought you came here to rest.

"On the contrary, to understand."

Penetrate the veils of the Mystery.

"Indeed."

So you are both the watcher and the watched?

"Seems that way."

The observer of the film and the film itself?

"Yep."

Why the separation?

"Oh my …"

Eyes widening.

"No, it can't be."

Uh huh.

"Just consciousness … being?"

Silence.

"I am a point of consciousness. Being."

Quietude.

Fingers brushing my temples.

You're not going to 'Aaargghh!' again, are you?

"Perhaps in a minute. What is beyond these films, stories, thoughts? What happens when they fall away?"

Genial giggle. *A fundamental question in your reality.*

"I am a point of consciousness ... thoughts in motion ..."

True.

"I am the thinker and the thoughts ..."

What if you are just the thoughts?

"Then who is the thinker?"

I wonder.

"Aaargghh!"

Need space? More time?

"Those do not exist."

Vision hazy. Slurring. What's happening to me?

She lays me down on the cashmere blanket. The night stars illuminate the darkest heavens. A fluorescent green glow appears out of nowhere, filling the atmosphere at incredible speed. Aurora borealis. The spectacular northern lights. I weep at its magnificence.

Gazing at all the thoughts. Streams of knowledge. Wisps of wisdom. Tumultuous whispers and endless conversations. So many beings. Are we not thinkers? Are we not even witnesses? Are we all just thoughts?

Taking a deep breath. I am not going down this avenue. Not yet anyway.

Surveying the exquisite glimmering stars. Why is it that every time I start to understand, every time I finally grasp a concept, a new transition appears?

A point of consciousness experiencing a wave of thought. Am I not the thinker?

The question remains unanswered by the knowledge bank.

Perhaps I am simply not ready.

* * *

"M"

You called?

"I need a mission."

Why?

"I'm apprehensive about the next transition."

You reached a plateau.

"Plateau?"

In your climb to the mountaintop.

"Is that normal?"

There's only so much you can experience in this dimension.

"Other beings plateau too?"

Every being in this dimension approaches the threshold.

"What threshold?"

Are you listening to yourself?

"Um ..."

Who's in charge of your journey?

"I'm not sure anymore."

As long as you are the thinker ...

"I am captain of the ship."

So where's the threshold?

"In my mind, my consciousness."

And what directs your journey?

"Intention."

The key that fits all locks.

"I am consciousness and intention directs my journey."

Precisely.

"That's like a mantra, isn't it?"

Sage nod.

You really don't need me anymore.

"I don't?"

I cannot lead you past this threshold.

"Why not?"

All beings in this reality reach a similar boundary.

"Oh, I see …"

Hence, we are still here.

"You face a fundamental question too."

We all do. Every being at every level.

"What now?"

You asking me?

"Wait a minute. Apart from new arrivals, we all have access to the knowledge bank. We operate within a collective consciousness. Yet we are all stuck here."

Except those that have transitioned to the next dimension.

"Is that the only transition remaining?"

Of course not.

I give her a quizzical stare.

"What aren't you telling me?"

Silence.

Here we go again.

Cast my mind back to a previous conversation.

"You once told me: *The door is located within each point of consciousness. Behind that door is the Light that every being seeks.*"

Ah, the teachings are not lost.

"All consciousness journeys toward the Light."

Directly or circumspectly.

"Is there a path?"

Two paths.

"Tell me."

Awareness.

Long pause.

"And ..."

Love.

"That's it?"

Yep.

"Hmm ... I have focused almost entirely on Awareness since I left Earth."

You have indeed.

"And now I have plateaued."

Uh huh.

"So I guess that leaves Love."

That's a whole other adventure.

"What is Love?"

Huge smile. *A fundamental question –*

"Of course it is."

Well, what's the answer?

"Kindness, giving, service ..."

Yes.

"Focus on the other."

In one word?

"Um ..."

Staring at the ground.

"Altruism."

Meaning?

"Selfless concern for the well-being of others."

Perfect.

"So what's the plan?"

You tell me.

"Could I become a Messenger?"

Thought you'd never ask.

"Really?"

Welcome to the next level.

"Ahem!"

Oh, alright. Welcome to the next perceptual point.

Beaming smile. Tender embrace.

* * *

A new phase begins. Part of me thinks I am going backward. Taking on another role. Averting my gaze from the coquettish Light. But I need a break. The next level of awareness seems too much to bear.

What were M's words? Ah, yes. *Your awareness expands only when you can handle it. You are supported by an ambience of love and freedom, and the occasional prompt, but the veils only drop when you are ready.*

I have to accept that another path beckons.

After some debate I turned down the position of Guardian. I have no interest in other worlds. Leave that to the adventurous spirits. I like it here. Is this heaven? May as well be. Abundant Light and Love permeate the fabric of this dimension. It's a wonderful place to exist. Feels like home.

The great thing about being a Messenger is that I can move freely between various realities. Although my primary function is to support and guide, I am also expected to assist beings facing reality transitions. Sometimes this means escorting a point of consciousness from one physical world to another, sometimes from one dimension to another. The destination is contingent on the being's evolution, awareness and readiness. It is not up to me. I simply hold their hand as they cross into uncertainty.

The key thing to remember is that each being is viewing All That Is through its own perceptual point. I quickly learn to speak the 'language of perspective'. It's a selfless action. My thoughts and words are tailored to each being's viewpoint. Other than that, there is nothing more I can do.

In a sense, this is a 'waiting game' and patience is a Messenger's greatest virtue. In fact, ruminating on the idea of patience indicates a misunderstanding about evolution, awareness and readiness.

The deeper you immerse into Love, the more concepts like tolerance, patience and empathy fall away. The latter are mere stepping stones on the path of Love. Beacons for those beings who haven't quite grasped the nature of Love.

Over time, even the word 'altruism' loses its flavour. 'Selfless concern for the well-being of others'. What meaning does that hold when your self is disappearing? When your life is completely devoted to the other?

Love erodes and destroys the self. It is a candle flame that burns the consciousness. The more I serve and abandon myself to Love, the deeper I am pulled into that flame. I wonder where it all ends.

I am standing near the fountain, admiring the cohort of new arrivals. A melange of disorientation, sadness, joy and wide-eyed wonder. Ambling over to ascertain which entity needs my assistance.

"Chuya." A hand quickly extends.

I cheerfully greet the forthright entity.

"Call me O."

"O?"

"Short for Old Sage. Names don't mean much around here."

"How do I summon others?"

"Just think about them and they appear."

"Ok."

I wave toward the path and start walking. He hurries after me.

"So, you going to show me the ropes?"

"Ropes?"

"Yeah. How things operate."

I shrug and smile.

"You create your own reality. The only limit is your imagination."

"I can levitate? Fly?"

"If you choose."

In a blink he is gone. A soaring condor cavorting across the skies. Take a deep breath. May as well join him. Within moments a huge eagle cruises alongside. Wingtip to wingtip we hover in the warm trade winds. Then we begin to test the limits of our minds. Steep vertical descent into an outside loop. Not even a feather is ruffled. Impressive.

Time to crank it up a notch.

Cuban Eight: Figure 8 rotated on its side, using loops and half rolls. He follows me flawlessly. Standard Roll: Wings rotating around the body. No problem. Barrel Roll: Flying straight while rotating around an imaginary barrel. Immaculate. Vertical Up: Thrusting the body to a 90 degree angle then straight and level, without losing speed or altitude. Perfection.

We land on the ground a couple of hours later. It's quiet. A marvellous sunset is forming. Soon the world is painted in brushstrokes of maroon and glimmering gold. Chuya stares, mouth agape.

Eventually he asks "Is that you?"

"Yeah. It's fun when you get the hang of it."

"Beautiful."

"Hey, where did you learn to fly like that?"

"Surfing inside a condor's consciousness."

"Meaning?"

He smiles. "I was a shaman on Earth. Peru was my home. Shamans walk in the energy worlds."

Shaman Chuya. How interesting.

"What brings you here?"

"It was my time. The next world was calling."

"Sounds like an easy transition."

"Long overdue."

"Really?"

"Lost my wife and children. Finished my lessons. Let go of service."

"Service?"

"I was a Q'ero shaman. Taught the principles of love, impeccability (mierkacitelność) and reciprocity." (wzajemność)

"Aha."

"With a deft sprinkling of magic."

Hmm … that's another world.

"I used to sprinkle cocoa powder on cappuccinos."

(doúeklíwie)
He looks at me inquisitively then bursts into laughter.

Hand rests on my shoulder. Radiant smile. "You and I are going to get along just fine."

I gaze at this mystical shaman. Confident and easy-going. Requiring only the lightest touch of mentorship. Seems he is already at home.

Curious feeling that he might teach me a thing or two.

* * *

Our morning starts with a speed test. Eagle and condor side by side, pushing the boundaries of the heavens. Clouds, wisps, thin blue air … just how fast can we go? Eventually everything blurs. Impossible to see. Finest streaks.

A loud craaack!

Stunned, I slowly spread my wings.

Chuya hovers next to me. "What happened?"

Accessing the knowledge bank. Unavailable. "No idea."

"Where are we?"

"I don't know."

There is nothing but the whitest bright light surrounding us.

I glance at my protégé. "Can you manifest any thought-forms?"

"Uh uh."

"Me neither."

Disorienting. Unable to ascertain direction. Zero reference points.

Where is M? Calling her. She does not appear.

In the distance a tiny speck. Luminous colours. Green, silver and gold.

Ah, the hummingbird. Wings buzzing. Circling us. Dark eyes staring.

Right on time. Let's begin.

Chuya seems elated. Does he know the hummingbird?

Impertinently, I ask "You going to teach us to fly?"

Penetrating gaze.

Old Sage, you of all beings should know.

"Know what?"

The Space Between.

I shrug.

The underlying fabric of existence.

Chuya looks at me kindly. "The Light."

"Oh."

Now, stretch your wings.

"What?"

Silent waiting.

I watch Chuya struggling for a while. Why can't he move?

It is soon evident that we are both immobilised.

Whisper from the shaman. "Do we have bodies?"

"Not really. They are manifestations of thought."

"How were we flying?"

"Our thoughts were flying."

"We weren't going anywhere?"

I shake my head.

He stares at me. "The only limit is imagination."

"Yes."

"Is our dimension a place?"

"No."

Recalling the words of M.

"A dimension is not a place. You are not travelling through distance when you transition."

"What is a dimension?"

"Dimensions are expressions of Life. As you shift your consciousness, you can step into various dimensions."

Long pause. Slow blink.

Chuya disappears.

"What the –?"

You're a little slow on the uptake.

"Where did he go?"

To visit his wife and children.

"How? Where?"

In another dimension.

Quietude settles.

Backtrack. Everything is consciousness. Dimensions are consciousness. I am consciousness. I have no body. I am unmoving. Only my consciousness shifts.

"Everything is consciousness."

Yes.

"Intention. The key that fits all locks."

Indeed.

My turn to blink. Eyes widening. Oh!

I am surfing along radiant undulating waves. Hard to navigate. It's all consciousness. Express my intention. Waves forming into a circle ... now a long tunnel ... myriad doors ... brightest colours ... noise ... intense scchhh!

Ah. Chuya got it before me. No limits. Perhaps he had prior experience.

I am flying across wild and bright geometry and experiencing one mind-boggling dimension after another. Each doorway is a portal into unseen colours, unheard sounds and fantastical expressions of life. The beings I meet are intelligent, kind, inquisitive, spiritual, fun, strange, bizarre, absurd and extraordinary.

In truth, I am neither flying nor moving. My consciousness is moving. My awareness is expanding. My perceptual points are shifting.

Luminous glow of the hummingbird. Strange buzzing.

"I finally understand."

Faint hint of a smile.

"Am I still bound by the Three Immutable Laws?"

Are you still a Messenger?

Perfunctory ponder.

"I guess not."

A free agent?

"Yes."

en ote
A wise protégé once revealed his code: Power. Virtue. Responsibility.

"Who was that?"

The Time Lord. It's a whole other story.

"Aha."

(ožyιvíc)

Absorb that code. Enliven it.

I nod respectfully.

Moment's hesitation. Insightful stare.

"What is it?"

A faint glimmer of destiny.

"Meaning?"

Potential catalyst.

We gaze at each other awhile. The eyes glint mysteriously.

Then it abruptly flits into a dazzling stream of light and disappears.

Once again, a transition has left me with bewildering questions.

What is a catalyst? Who is the hummingbird? Why is it so enigmatic and annoying?

Closing my eyes and shifting my consciousness. Arrive in the green-tinged world.

I look around and smile. Is this heaven? I think so.

Glad to be home.

* * *

Hey!

"M"

What happened? You fell off the grid.

"I did?"

Thought I heard a faint whisper but couldn't find you.

"I was not part of the collective consciousness?"

Only a hint of you. A vague outline.

"How peculiar."

I wonder. Do I leave a footprint in every dimension I visit?

Where were you?

"Everywhere."

Another transition?

"I guess."

Never seen such progress.

"Thing is, I'm not progressing."

You're not?

Insouciant shrug. "There is nowhere to go, nothing to do."

Touché.

"My awareness expands."

Your lifetimes have prepared you well.

"True."

The less ideology you carry, the clearer your perceptual filters.

"The veils of perception fall."

Inspiring.

"The answer lies not in seeking. Rather in being."

You are starting to sound like a teacher.

"Is there anything to teach?"

A gracious whisper?

"I can only be."

Every step is on the path.

Prescient laughter. "There is no path."

The way is within?

"I am the way. You are the way."

She sits cross-legged on the viridescent grass. Plucks a daisy and peruses the white petals. Silently contemplating.

Eventually, *Old Sage, what has happened to you?*

"I am thought. Everything is Thought."

Wow. You are disappearing before me.

"The only limit is your imagination."

I guess you will be leaving soon.

My hand rests gently on her shoulder.

"The self plans. The self dreams. The self grieves."

You are a true inspiration.

"Your awareness expands when you can handle it. The veil drops when you are ready."

Broad smile. *My words?*

"Indeed."

How does Love fit into all this?

"Every coin has two sides."

What are you saying?

"Awareness and Love."

obscure - difficult to understand

The wiser you become, the more abstruse the teachings.

zawity

I am beginning to shimmer. It's a comfortable way to say goodbye.

migotać

"Think of me and I will appear."

I'm going to miss you.

Deferential bow.

Away.

* * *

It's a new world. A different reality.

I never left the green-tinged heaven. It simply phased out of my perception.

It's taken a while for this truth to sink in: I don't move. Never have. Never will.

Only my awareness shifts. My perceptual points expand.

I suppose you could call it 'vibration'. Perhaps the apt description is 'essence signature'. But those are spatial terms to assist less-expanded forms of consciousness.

In truth, I am consciousness. I am thought. I exist among Thought. I surf among Thought. Intention is the key and imagination demarcates the limits.

I have come so far from cappuccino-making Joe. Smiling silently. 'Cuppa Joe'. Has a nice ring to it. Maybe I will reincarnate in that form.

So, all 'progress' is not defined by what you gain, rather by what you lose. It is a subtle and steady erosion of the self, of the ego, of the I. The slow disappearance of self-development, self-fulfilment, self-identity and self-aggrandisement.

It is a constant letting go. A gradual immersion into your true nature – pure consciousness. Flowing thought.

Everything prior to that is a dream.

In truth, everything is a dream.

"Who are you?"

Jonathan.

"Why?"

The hummingbird sent me.

"Oh."

Heard you like to fly.

"I do."

Up for a challenge?

"Bring it."

I take my usual form. Golden eagle.

Alongside me, feather-tips barely touching mine, outstretched shimmering white wings. Small bird, impressive span.

A series of deft aeronautic manoeuvres. Reverse Half Cuban Eight. Craaack! Hammerhead. Craaack! Split S. Craaack! English Bunt. Craaack! Inverted Spin. Craaack!

Flawless execution. Perfect formation. Continually shifting realities.

I stretch and yawn then fall into a Lazy Eight.

"How many doors do you intend to enter?"

How many can you handle?

The afternoon slips past.

Doorway after doorway.

Dimension after dimension.

Fatigue begins to grip me.

What is his purpose? Dizzy. Tired.

You could spend lifetimes visiting all these worlds.

So many ... thoughts ... concepts ... ideas ... need rest ...

Fading on me?

"What's the ... hurry?"

I collapse on a huge palm frond. Soft breeze swaying my weary –

Body?

Twinkling stars. Dark heavens.

You're not going to tell me you have a body.

"Of course not!" I snap.

My response startles me.

What's the problem?

"Uh ..."

Too much to process?

I nod carefully.

You have your whole life ahead of you.

"Yep ..."

He turns to leave.

Catch you in another lifetime.

Pull myself together. Try to focus.

"Wait …"

Backward glance. Curious glint in the eye.

Shaking my foggy mind.

Throws an enormous orange into the air. Floats above me.

Did you have this fruit on Earth?

"Yes."

You peel it. Break it into segments.

"Uh huh."

Takes time to view each segment.

I stare at the enigmatic bird.

"True."

Let's slice the fruit across the horizontal axis.

Half an orange floats before me.

Stand in the centre of the orange.

Shifting my consciousness.

What do you see?

"Every segment at once."

He smiles mischievously.

A simple change in perspective.

I survey the juicy triangles.

"And this relates ... how?"

You'll work it out.

"Um ..."

Studiously observing me.

"All That Is ... relatively infinite ..."

Yeah ...

"I am free to surf it forever ..."

Mmm ...

"Space does not exist ..."

Jonathan's turn to yawn.

"Dimensions are not places ..."

He stretches and flaps his wings.

Come on. Where's the slow blink?

I blink slowly.

"Am I everywhere at once?"

Everywhere and everywhen.

"Why the limitations?"

Exactly!

"Open my awareness. Adjust my perceptual point."

As always, up to you.

Sudden rush of energy and information.

Tremendous whirring sound.

Wait for it …

Deluge of thought. Cascade of consciousness.

Wait for it …

"Aaargghh!" I hear my ecstatic shout.

Stunned. Staring. Absorbing. Immersion.

Profound quietude. Surreal silence.

Oh my … All That Is …

Beautiful, yes?

Words flail uselessly.

Awesome. Everything. Existence. Life.

"Where is this centre point?"

Where? When? What?

"Uh … no space, no time."

Beyond one point.

Aha.

"Here Now."

Yes.

Delicious sacred sensations enveloping me.

"What is the energy of Creation?"

You know the answer.

"Love."

Indeed.

I bow in gratitude.

Shimmering white wings begin to ripple.

He smiles seraphically.

My work is done.

"Nowhere to go, nothing to do."

Soft laughter. He disappears.

* * *

I wake up hours later. Or did I just fade away for a while?

Oh, this journey of life. Fascinating. It starts wherever you are. Yes, here now.

Every day, every moment, the choices you make dictate your reality.

Your perceptions dictate your reality. In fact, you are your perceptions.

The secret is to loosen your tight grip on the world. Let go the rigid ideologies and belief systems. Open your mind and consciousness to the endless possibilities.

All That Is beckons you. It desires that you embrace it. That you relinquish, surrender, dive in, explore, flow.

I have become part of Everything, of Existence, of Life. In fact, I was never separate. I am thought, weaved with all Thought. I am consciousness, melded with all Consciousness.

One thing is crystal clear. The deeper into Consciousness you proceed, the more useless become your words. All terms are mere reference points tailored to your level of awareness. The illusory concepts of ego, space, time and subjectivity simply assist your limited perceptions.

Nothing is separate. There is only Thought. There is only Consciousness. You are That.

And yet ... something is itching me ...

I sense one last veil ... a final curtain to draw back ...

Strange. I have never been a seeker. More interested in living.

This is different. Something is seeking me.

Only one option.

To surf All That Is.

To flow in the River of Life.

To survey Existence from Here Now.

An immense project.

"H"

H?

"Seems we prefer letters to names."

The luminous wings glow brightly.

Mind if I tag along?

"Be my guest."

Any form preference?

"You tired of being a hummingbird?"

Instantly becomes a spark of brilliant light. Have to shield my perception awhile. Eventually I adjust.

"Why is your energy so intense?"

Indistinct shrug. *It's the Light.*

I manifest as pure energy. My form appears cloudy in comparison.

"You standing in a different place to me?"

My consciousness has a different perceptual position.

"Touché. A more accurate description."

Let's get started. Lead the way.

"Just jump?"

Yep.

Ok. Earth is a familiar place.

SHIFTING MY CONSCIOUSNESS.

It's a beach in Cape Town, South Africa.

Teacher. Long white hair, almond-shaped piercing blue eyes.

Even though our energy is undetectable by the human student, I notice the teacher quietly acknowledging us. Evidently he can see into the multi-dimensions. Intriguing. Who is he?

The hummingbird and I settle, for the most part, as invisible spectators. We watch and listen.

Dozens of seagulls congregate, forming a huge circle. Soon more of them pour in and the circle becomes thick and dark. The student is staring into the sky.

Teacher: *This is your first lesson and the most important one. Pay close attention. Those seagulls have formed together in a special way. Is there anything in the circle?*

Student: "No, it's just sky. The same bright blue sky that is on the outside of the circle. Everything is just sky but those birds have created a circle."

Teacher: *Tell me what you see. Is there anything but the sky and the gulls?*

Student: "There is nothing but the sky and the gulls."

Teacher: *What about the circle that the gulls appear to have formed? Does the circle have an identity or a personality of its own? Does it actually exist on its own, independently of the gulls?*

Student: "No, of course not. There is just sky and an illusion of a circle formed by the gulls. As soon as the gulls fly away that circle will be part of the sky again."

Teacher: *Excellent. No matter what anyone tells you or how things may appear, remember: that circle does not really exist. It is all sky, which is obvious when we remove the birds.*

The ocean waves are making that exquisite swooshing sound. A gentle breeze is teasing the golden-white sand. The sun shimmers brightly.

I turn to the hummingbird.

"Those seem like advanced lessons for a human."

Perspicacious laughter.

How many students are present?

"What do you mean?"

Are you paying attention?

I gaze deeper into Existence.

"Teaching across many dimensions."

Yep.

"Conversing in numerous worlds."

Are you still holding onto limitations?

Wow. Is it possible? Am I not entirely free?

The veils of perception.

SHIFTING MY CONSCIOUSNESS.

Sun Island, The Maldives. This teacher has a fondness for oceans. He is looking across the water at the clear blue sky. The student follows his gaze.

Teacher: *Those small seabirds with the pure white plumage are called White Terns.*

Student: "Yep, I see them."

Teacher: *Are those birds or merely expressions of Life?*

Student: "I don't know."

Teacher: *Have you ever watched a film, and for a few moments become so immersed in the story that you forgot who you are and where you are?*

Student: "Yes, of course."

Teacher: *How did you wake up? How did you return to reality?*

Student: "You just become aware that you are watching a story. You return to reality."

Teacher: *What if you are just a story? And your appearance? Your beliefs? Your values? What if these are all just stories?*

Student: "If these are all just stories, then at some point I will realise I am completely immersed in the film and wake up. I will remember who I am and where I am."

The hummingbird surveys me serenely.

"What is it?"

Why did you bring us here?

"I don't know. Maybe the teaching is seeking me."

Wise words, young protégé.

I laugh softly. Old Sage, young protégé. Guess we are all learning.

Are you learning?

"I think so."

Tell me.

"I am thought. I am part of Thought. I am immersed in Thought."

The birds in the sky.

"Yes …"

Weaved into the film.

"Uh …"

Lost in the stories.

"Are we approaching a transition?"

Up to you.

"What's behind all the stories? Beyond all the thoughts?"

The hummingbird's light-hearted smile tickles my energy.

The most fundamental question in your reality.

Should have seen that coming.

I crouch over a pink Sweetheart rose and breathe in the delicious scent. Is there something behind the stories? Beyond all Thought?

Makes no sense. Thought behind Thought? Ever more stories? But it's still all Thought. Consciousness is Consciousness is Consciousness.

Not something. Someone.

"Thinker?"

Silent stare.

"Storyteller?"

Subtle nod.

"There's a Being behind all this?"

That's for you to discover.

How delightfully cryptic.

Over to you.

SHIFTING MY CONSCIOUSNESS.

Ryoan-ji Zen Garden in Kyoto, Japan. Śakra is speaking to Adam.

Teacher: *To answer your question: I am mortal. Everything that is created is mortal. This is the transient nature of creation. Only the underlying Source lives forever.*

Student: "Are you reading my mind?"

Teacher: *Everything is a thought-force. Your beliefs are a bit antiquated so you operate on a limited wavelength. In time this will change.*

Student: "What beliefs?"

Teacher: *Do you believe you are just a body? Or a mind? What if you are consciousness? What if you are expressed everywhere and everywhen at the same time? What if there are no past lives but simply one life expressed across multiple dimensions? What if beings in other dimensions are just varying expressions of you?*

SHIFTING MY CONSCIOUSNESS.

Ulundi, in the province of KwaZulu-Natal, South Africa. Iboga and Śakra are sitting with Adam in the shade of the Amarula tree.

Teacher: "God is the Source, the underlying Is-ness, the Creator of everything. A deep ocean that gives rise to infinite waves. Your reality is merely one of these waves."

Teacher: *All life is a journey, a progression and a gradual return to the Source.*

The hummingbird flutters its wings wildly.

Probably a cue.

"Under the infinite waves is a deep ocean."

Yes.

"A being called God manifests all Thought."

Patient nod.

"God is the creator of Everything."

Yep.

"Like the waves return to the ocean, all thoughts and consciousness return to the Source."

Indeed.

I stare into the bright blue African sky. A sunbird is slowly preening itself in the Amarula. Soon it descends and dances around my feet. Hmm …

"Why does God create?"

Why don't you find out?

SHIFTING MY CONSCIOUSNESS.

Cortile della Pigna, Vatican City, Rome. Ra puts his hand on Adam's shoulder.

Teacher: *The greatest truth you will ever know is that Life is breathing. In this very moment, in the Now, there is a simultaneous In-Breath and Out-Breath. The Source manifests countless dimensions and infinite realities – the Out-Breath, the act of creation. And all of creation flows back to the Source – the In-Breath, the return and dissolution. This is the flow of Life.*

Ok. I understand that part. Deeper explanation required.

SHIFTING MY CONSCIOUSNESS.

Golden Temple, Amritsar, Punjab, India. Sikh Nanak is making the short walk to the temple.

Teacher: "Adi means 'primordial' and Shakti means 'power'. So Adi Shakti means Primordial Power of God. There exists nothing but God and his Shakti. God is the unmanifested observer and she is the embodiment of his dreams. She creates all the universes with her endless love. She in fact *is* the creation. All of creation is merely a beautiful cloak to wrap God in and make him visible."

Teacher: "Shakti is infinite. If you swim in her holy waters, you will be lost and found, lost and found, lost and found. It is an adventure with no end. Until you reunite with God."

I take a deep breath.

The hummingbird smiles.

"God is the underlying Source, the unmanifested Being, the invisible Observer. The Shakti element of God manifests Creation so that God may observe Itself."

Almost there.

"God creates in order to know Aliveness."

Excellent.

"Imagine you are alone on a desert island. You are aware and conscious, but there is no one to reflect your consciousness. No one to mirror or manifest your thoughts. Creation serves as a mirror and manifestation for God."

Useful analogy. Are you done?

"Wait. I need more information."

SHIFTING MY CONSCIOUSNESS.

Inside the caves of Uluru (aka Ayers rock), Australia. Śakra engages an audience.

Teacher: *There are two aspects to Life. The one is the underlying Source, the almost ubiquitous unmanifested Field of Dreams. This is represented by the god Shiva, the harbinger of death. The other is the infinite realities, the manifested dreams. This is represented by the goddess Shakti, who is both the creative force and the creation.*

The Source by its very nature is invisible and impossible to encounter without experiencing your own death. Everything that is created will eventually dissolve into the Source. This is the inevitable role of Shiva.

Shakti is the one who weaves the magic cloth, who spins the universal web, who brings the dreams to life. She is the manifestation of the Source, effectively rendering the Source visible to itself.

Shiva and Shakti are the greatest Lovers. Love is when Life meets itself through creation. Love is when Life returns home to the Source. Life is breathing this Love in the eternal Now. Life is essentially one big orgasm of the Heart.

Student: "If there's an eternal Now, is there not an eternal Being?"

Teacher: *There is only One Consciousness and everything is a manifestation of that Consciousness. Everything that is manifested is still the One Consciousness. Everything that exists is a Thought of God but the Thoughts also are God. Everything is One. One Being, One Moment, One Breath.*

Student: "So Shiva and Shakti are one."

Teacher: *Shiva and Shakti are themselves merely Thoughts of God. There is only One Consciousness. The Source is faintly understood through its symbols and manifestations. To truly know the Source, you need to die to self and swim in the One Consciousness. This is called awakening or enlightenment.*

I vociferate a "Whoo hoo!"

The hummingbird watches me sagaciously.

"Aha! The crux of the matter."

I'm listening.

"The Source is the underlying unmanifested Is-ness. The Source creates through Love: the Out-Breath. Life is infinite Existence. Existence is a form of Love and Aliveness. Once Creation is done, it dissolves back into the Source: the In-Breath. All Life is the Breath of God."

True.

"Every being, every thought, every point of consciousness is a manifestation of God. Therefore every being, every thought, every point of consciousness is on the journey back to God."

Yes.

"There is only an eternal Now. One Being, One Moment, One Breath."

And the answer to the fundamental question?

I can almost touch it.

Just beyond my reach.

What is the answer?

Time to go surfing again.

SHIFTING MY CONSCIOUSNESS.

Chua Chua, Andes Mountains, Peru. Ah, the teacher with the long white hair and almond-shaped piercing blue eyes. The next level of the lesson.

Teacher: *What about the circle that the gulls appear to have formed? Does the circle have an identity or a personality of its own? Does it actually exist on its own, independently of the gulls?*

Student: "No, of course not. There is only sky and the illusion of a circle formed by the gulls. As soon as the gulls fly away that circle will simply disappear."

Teacher: *That circle appears real when there are so many birds. Who are you when all your thoughts have flown away?*

I watch the student slip into the Tunnel of Light. Pulsating vortex. Spiralling bright colours. Innumerable doors. Intensely loud scchhh!

Teacher: *Who are you without your thoughts and stories? What happens when you let go of all those birds? When you surrender?*

The student's consciousness is propelled toward the Light. Intense wrestling match. Dissolution of the ego. Ultimate capitulation. Deepest surrender. Submerged in the Light. Oneness. Revelation.

Student: I am God. I am All That Is. I am the Source of All. I am Is-ness, Source, Pure Consciousness, Pure Awareness, Light and Life. I am the existence of every possibility. I Am.

Wow.

"H?"

Yes?

"You knew all along."

I did.

"Why didn't you tell me?"

It's your journey.

SHIFTING MY CONSCIOUSNESS.

I am Joe. Leaving my physical body. Saying goodbye.

Huge pulsating vortex with spiralling bright colours and millions of doors. Intensely loud scchhh! Completely disorienting.

Michael grabs my arm. *Pay attention. Most people miss this part.*

We surf along the energy stream until a glowing portal appears. The most beautiful Light is just ahead of us. We step through the door into a green-tinged world.

Student: "Is this heaven?"

Teacher: *Really? Thought you were free of ideology.*

Student: "What happened to the Light?"

Teacher: *You are not ready for it. One step at a time.*

The hummingbird shimmers with ebullient laughter.

I sit on the grassy hill and manifest a glorious sunset. The Light was there all along. I was just not in the optimal state of awareness and readiness.

Trying to recall M's words. Oh yes. *Your awareness expands only when you can handle it. You are supported by an ambience of love and freedom, and the occasional prompt, but the veils only drop when you are ready.*

Deep breath. Exulted sigh.

Glance at the brilliant sparkling light.

"What now, hummer?"

As always, up to you.

* * *

The gentle swoosh of sapphire waves is soothing my weary consciousness.

A breeze softly cascades over the white-and-grey pebbles. I adore the Mediterranean Sea. Exquisite turquoise waters. Pine and cedar trees strewn along the coastline. Olive and fig trees dotting the surrounding hills. Paradisical.

There is something beyond Thought.

The Thinker Itself.

God.

The purveyor of all Thought.

I have observed the final transition.

The walk into the Light.

Complete immersion.

Ultimate surrender.

Pondering my state of awareness.

Am I ready for the final veil to drop?

What will ensue when my consciousness moves beyond Thought?

What will transpire when I meet the Thinker?

Will I cease to exist?

Has God been seeking me?

I gaze across the aquamarine water.

The waves are rising. Trees swaying inward. Hills curving.

What is happening? Who is doing this?

The scenery forms an enormous vortex.

Sea swirls along the edges and flows toward the end.

Suddenly I am tumbling along the turbulent tunnel.

Beneath the water, pulsating doors beckoning.

Each one a promise, a dream, a temptation.

Flailing, out of control, drawn, pulled.

Familiar green-silver-gold whirring.

You have a choice.

"I do?"

Always.

"Free will?"

Absolutely.

"Where am I going?"

Where do you want to go?

"The realities are infinite."

Yes they are.

"If I travel to the end, will I die?"

Who are you?

"Who am I?"

Insightful.

"You're always so much help."

It's your journey.

"Touché."

Decision time.

"Will you be here when I return?"

Are you coming back?

I sigh and leap into the Light.

Thought disappears.

Overwhelming Love permeates my being.

I become Love. I am Love.

I cry. I weep. I sob. I release. I let go.

No desire to move. Aeons could pass.

Floating. Immersion. Being. Love.

Rapturous. Euphoric. Blissful.

Ecstatic. Love. Love. Love.

Why unmoving?

"H?"

Yes?

"What are you doing here?"

Really? Is that the question?

"There's something deeper than Love?"

What you seek is seeking you.

"An enigma wrapped in a cryptogram."

The final veil is ready to drop.

Courage. Vulnerability. Surrender.

The last perceptual point shifts.

Nothing.

Emptiness.

Wait. This is not emptiness or nothing.

Blending with the Light. Dissolving into the Source.

Beyond all the forms and the illusions of infinite realities, there is nothing but pure unmanifested Consciousness. Nothing but Consciousness.

There is nothing but One Consciousness.

I am this One Consciousness.

I am the Creator of All.

I am Pure Awareness.

I am the Light.

I am God.

I am.

I am.

I am.

"I AM!"

The hummingbird gently alights on my shoulder.

Roisterous laughter pervades the Here Now.

"I AM."

"I AM."

"I AM."

* * *

I wake up on the Mediterranean beach.

The sun is setting and long shadows are dancing across the pebbles.

Pines are whispering to the tamarisks. Shimmering wavelets tease the shore.

Wordless, I gaze at the beautiful seascape.

Eventually a full moon rises, casting its silver cloak over the rippling water. Tiny white-tipped horses canter across the bay. Tranquillity caresses the treetops, trickles down the hills, then gently settles upon the ethereal terrain.

One question remains.

Why am I still here?

I know I Am yet I still exist.

You could ask me the same question.

"Why are you still here?"

It's all a choice.

"It is?"

You create your reality.

"Why did I choose to be here?"

That's the real question.

"Aha."

Time to go surfing?

"Indeed."

SHIFTING MY CONSCIOUSNESS.

Nepal, India. Gautama Buddha is talking to Indra.

Teacher: "Enlightenment is an experience of the Divine. It is the sinking and submerging of the illusory self into the Lake of Light until you are aware only of Consciousness. You are Consciousness. Everything is Consciousness and everything is a manifestation of the Source. This is the fun of illusory duality. I know I Am. Yet I find myself still expressed in this limited reality. Part human, part divine."

Student: "Wait a minute. Isn't it all a choice?"

Teacher: "Indeed. As long as I hold onto this sliver of personal consciousness, as long as that remains, I do not fully dissolve into the Light. That is my choice. One I make every moment."

Student: "What would happen if you let go?"

Teacher: "I would disappear from your reality. In fact, I would disappear from all realities. I would be the Source, the underlying unmanifested Is-ness."

I glance at the hummingbird.

"Seems we both made a choice."

Yep. Personal aliveness.

"Why?"

Usually for a mission.

"Really?"

There are few options at this level.

"You mean after awakening?"

Enlightenment.

"Options?"

Search.

SHIFTING MY CONSCIOUSNESS.

Avebury, near Marlborough, England.

It's the teacher with the long white hair and almond-shaped piercing blue eyes.

Student: "What are you doing here?"

Teacher: *I should be asking you that question.*

Student: "I Am. I don't know what I am doing in this reality anymore."

Teacher: *From where I am sitting, you have a few choices: You exit this reality and stay in the Light; you surf through different realities enjoying the great Dance of Life; or you stay in this reality and make a difference on this planet. These are the choices for every enlightened being.*

Student: "Is this what you meant by the second journey?"

Teacher: *Yes. Every experience you have ever had, and every moment of every lifetime, has been leading you toward enlightenment. Every being is treading the same path, making their own way toward the Light. Your second journey is the fun you have after enlightenment. It is, of course, not a journey, as there is nowhere to go. Your life now, as ever, is the result of the choices you make.*

I burst into laughter.

Peruse the hummingbird.

"So, what did you choose?"

I am a catalyst.

"Catalyst?"

Light of the highest order, agitating systems to the next level.

"Aha."

What will you choose?

"That, my friend, is a mystery."

Mediterranean breeze invigorating my being.

The sun is rising. It's a new day.

I have some choices to make.

Time to close my eyes.

Contemplate.

* * *

I decide to surf the innumerable realities.

The great Dance of Life.

Countless worlds.

Nothing to do. Nothing to achieve.

No agenda. No plan.

There never was anywhere to go.

So why start now?

It's just being.

Exploring the Thoughts.

Shining the Light.

Noticing the shifting of consciousness.

My presence is a simple reminder.

A shining beacon on the path.

The path that is no path.

Hmm … perhaps a few planets.

Arcturus.

Home of the Galactic Leaders.

Planet Mani, a magnificent blue-green gem.

The Pagoda, enormous multi-tiered building housing the Planetary Government.

Crystal Temple of Arcturus, home of the Galactic Government.

A secretive and intriguing Time Lord.

The mysterious Light Seer.

I move quietly, disturbing no one.

Invisible, undetectable.

A mere observer of worlds.

Yet she discerns me immediately.

Old Sage.

"Seer."

What are you doing?

Shake my head.

"Being."

You don't have a mission?

"No. Do I need one?"

Astute shrug.

Your essence has changed.

"True."

Old Sage is no longer a suitable name.

"What do you see?"

Light Walker.

I nod.

Being without a mission.

"And what is yours?"

To monitor and report the movement of consciousness toward the Light.

"Aha."

Been watching you for a long time.

"Of course."

I also update the Council of Light about the condition of the Time Lord.

"Intriguing being."

You have no idea.

"One in every galaxy?"

Indeed.

I gaze at this fascinating entity.

So, Light Walker, what's the plan?

"Travel, explore, live."

Interesting.

"Want some company?"

Can you handle it?

Laughter enfolds me.

"What's there to handle?"

Witnessing, observing.

"Stressful?"

It's a quiet life.

"Sounds perfect."

The perspective of the Light Seer is enthralling. Peering into multitudinous dimensions and realities, we watch myriad expressions of Life journeying toward the Source.

Triumphs, tragedies, successes and failures. Love gained and lost. Ego aggrandisement and gradual dissolution. The frustration of decay and death. Impending annihilation of the self.

The constant choices. Choices, choices, choices.

Flow of essences to the next perceptual point.

Transition upon transition.

"How long, Seer?"

Aeons is an answer.

"In truth?"

Here Now.

"The abode of Time Lords and Light Seers."

And Light Walkers.

"Touché."

The occasional visitor too.

I smile.

"Policy of non-interference?"

Always.

"Gentle hints."

Yes.

"Tender prompts."

Of course.

"Is it difficult to just watch?"

You get used to it.

"No temptations?"

More harm is done by interfering.

"It's about free will."

True.

"Captain of the ship."

Self-determination.

"Awareness and readiness."

Arcturians have a saying …

"I'm listening."

Interference is perilous.

I nod quietly.

Except for that hummingbird.

"Old hummer?"

Yeah. It's so …

"Annoying?"

We fall into raucous laughter.

Exceptionally powerful.

"Catalyst in the system."

Necessary at times.

"Avatar of the Light."

That darn hummingbird.

I take a moment and close my eyes.

This marvellous interaction of Light Beings.

A finesse of puzzle pieces moving fluidly together.

Can't help but wonder if it's supremely orchestrated.

You know the Answer.

"H!"

Yep.

"We were just talking about you."

I heard.

"Oh."

You want to see how powerful?

"Uh ... ok."

It flexes its tiny wings.

Almighty shudder travels down the Tunnel of Light.

The ocean ebbs and flows. A huge ripple pummels toward us.

One Light Seer report coming up.

Enthralled, I listen to her words.

Summarise.

Immense movement of consciousness toward the Light.

Indeed.

"Impressive. How did you do that?"

What's the Answer?

"Huh?"

Silent stare.

Hmm. I've been to the end and back. Must know this.

"Um ..."

Tremulous cogitation.

"Everything is a Thought of God."

Hint of a smile.

And what is power?

Quietude.

Ah.

"The concentration of Thought."

Yes.

"The amount of God focused in a particular point."

Exactly.

"You have more God in you?"

I am God.

Scrutinising the hovering being.

Enigmatic bundle of luminous joy.

"I am God too."

You are.

Frustrating.

"Why don't you just say it?"

Teachers offer hints.

"Free will. Awareness. Readiness."

As always.

"Intention?"

The key that fits all locks.

"I need some downtime."

Something to process?

"You know it."

Curious glint in its dark eyes.

The green-gold wings stretch and flutter.

Later.

* * *

I stay with the Light Seer for a long time.

She seems blissed out doing her work.

Guess it's the call of her heart.

I realise now that my nature is unchanging.

Sure, there is more Light in me.

I am the Light.

I am God.

My way of living is still the same.

I have no desire to chase, seek or achieve.

For me, it's always about being.

Existence. Life. Here. Now.

Celebration. Presence. Gratitude.

At this level, the ultimate choice is simple:

Dissolution into the Light with zero personal existence.

Maintain the sliver of personal consciousness while being in the Light.

Personal existence versus Source existence.

If I hold onto this point of consciousness, there are other choices:

Do nothing and just be.

Surf the realities and play.

Find a mission and take action.

The hummingbird has a mission.

The Time Lord has a mission.

The Light Seer has a mission.

I take a deep breath and sigh.

The Thoughts of God are infinite.

It would take eternity to explore those dreams.

I wonder what happened to Chuya?

Instantly a gorgeous purple world appears.

Serene shades of mauve splashed across a soft landscape.

A lilac sun hovering above the horizon.

I amble through the undulating trees.

The smell of wood smoke.

Family seated around a campfire.

A man with black hair and deeply tanned face.

Beaming smile.

"O? Is that you?"

I bow courteously.

Huge embrace.

"Welcome to our reality."

"Thank you."

"Never thought I'd see you again."

Subdued shrug.

"Wanted to see how your life turned out."

He waves his hand.

"Well, this is it."

Introduces his wife and children. Brief tour of home.

I scratch my head pensively. Stare at the ground.

"What's up, O?"

"Why did you choose this reality?"

He motions toward a tree stump and sits alongside me.

Ornate stick in hand, sketching in the pink-hued sand.

"My life on Earth was dedicated to Love. The connectedness of all things. Living in service."

"Yes, I remember."

"I followed my heart's calling. The beckoning of my spirit."

"Uh huh."

"Fought the good fight. Destroyed the dark lattice."

The battle of Machu Picchu enters my mind.

I smile. "Legendary."

"At considerable personal cost."

"Your family."

I notice the rippling hearts drawn in the sand.

Chuya gazes into my eyes.

"When I met you, Old Sage, I learned that I was free."

"It's all about choices."

"Exactly."

He throws the stick into the bushes.

"My mission was fulfilled. I laid down the mantle of service. Went to find my family."

A solitary tear streams down his cheek.

"This is all I need."

Warm feeling rising in my heart.

Something stirring in my consciousness.

I shake his hand jubilantly.

"Well done, my friend."

We sit quietly and regard the dying fire.

The embers glow deep orange.

Finally he asks "And what about you, Old Sage?"

Sensing a shift in me ... still not clear ...

"So many transitions. Unsure."

"It'll come to you."

A few leaves and twigs create a sparkling flame.

Fetches a couple of small logs. Stokes the fire.

"Stay a while?"

I nod happily.

Wonderful feeling. Family. Loved ones. Togetherness.

Peaceful fulfilled existence.

Home.

* * *

All these beings I have met.

Each one a pointer, a way-shower.

Beacons on the path of Light.

Appearing and disappearing.

Leaving me with inevitable choices.

Everything in life is up to me.

I am the captain of my ship.

The steadfast helmsman.

My journey has been long.

Intense. Insightful.

Ongoing revelations.

The veils have dropped.

Here I am.

In the sky a flock of squawking and screeching birds.

Staring at the dazzling array of colours.

Abyssinian Lovebirds

Gold-Breasted Waxbills

Emerald Toucanets

Bare-Eyed Cockatoos

Rainbow Lories

Blue-and-Gold Macaws

Yellow-Headed Amazon Parrots

Golden-Mantled Rosellas

Jenday Conures

Immense dark clouds fill the heavens.

Tremendous rumbling. Shuddering wind.

Who is creating this?

Shard of sunlight pierces the ominousness.

Expansion of brilliant light.

Descending from on high, arms stretched wide.

It's the teacher with the long white hair and almond-shaped piercing blue eyes.

Bare feet touching the ground.

Wow.

You like the dramatic entrance?

"Uh … yeah."

He bursts into laughter.

Don't take it too seriously.

"Um … ok."

You need to have fun.

"Fun?"

Play.

"Play?"

More laughter.

You sound like those Amazon parrots.

"I do?"

Hmm ... it's lost on me.

Hand rests on my shoulder.

Dizzying sensation. Extraordinary peace flows into my being.

Penetrating gaze.

Are you a creator?

"I am the Creator."

Then create!

He sweeps his hand across the sky.

I watch in awe as dozens of psychedelic birds paint a spectacular mural.

Total immersion in shimmering flecks and strokes.

Tripping and flowing in ecstatic beauty.

Overwhelming splendour.

Exquisiteness.

Magnificent.

You know the Answer.

"I do."

There is nothing more to teach you.

"Really?"

All that remains is –

"Choices."

Indeed.

Slow nod.

I rub my chin and reflect awhile.

It seems that the same rules apply at every level … at every existential point …

Evolution of consciousness.

Non-interference.

Awareness.

Readiness.

Free will.

Choices.

A seagull flies overhead. It suddenly breaks into a series of aeronautic manoeuvres. I watch, entranced.

Self-determination.

"Yeah."

Reality creation.

"Yep."

Manifesting your essence.

"Uh huh."

Following your Heart Song.

"Absolutely."

Piercing blue eyes staring at me.

The veils have dropped.

"Unravelled the Mystery."

I say you are free.

"Who are you?"

Serene laughter echoes through the heavens.

I say You are Free!

Brilliant blazing light.

He is gone.

* * *

I am left alone with my thoughts.

A personal sliver of consciousness intermingled with All That Is.

Journeyed to the end of my world.

Beyond all the realities.

Discovered the Light.

Deep realisation.

The most fundamental question:

"What do I choose?"

Contemplative pause.

Gentle swoosh of sapphire waves.

Peace. Bliss. Joy. Freedom.

It's all so simple.

Just ask yourself:

"What am I holding?"

"What ideologies limit my perception?"

"What beliefs hinder my awareness?"

"What can I let go?"

Everything you need to know is hidden inside you.

There are no secrets you can't uncover.

No truth that can't be revealed.

When you discover your true nature ...

When you journey through the Mystery ...

When the veils drop ...

You discover that You are Free.

Oh.

That's what he meant.

Wait a minute.

I am free.

I am free!

Free to choose.

Free to express.

Free to live.

Free to be.

I am free!

Do I need a mission?

Do I need to preach?

Do I need to convert?

Do I need to point the way?

Trying to recall a conversation with M.

Oh yes ...

Why chase slivers of light? The Light you seek is inside you.

"Aha."

The door is located within each point of consciousness.

"It was there all along?"

Behind that door is the Light that every being seeks.

"Who can show us the door? Guardians? Messengers?"

Those who have already walked through the door. The enlightened ones.

"How can we identify them?"

They exude a radiant Light. They walk in deep peace, joy and bliss.

"Are they all teachers and guides?"

Recluses. Painters. Carpenters. Aeroplane mechanics. Philanthropists. Writers. Teachers.

"What about the teachings?"

Words are just seeds. The Light is the answer.

"Are there many enlightened ones?"

A handful in each reality.

"Why so few?"

They don't have to manifest anymore.

"Why do they stay?"

Those who remain made a choice.

"What choice?"

Love.

Ethereal sunbeams illuminate my world.

Crouching to admire a vermilion rose.

Gently caressing its delicate petals.

I blink slowly.

The final piece of the puzzle.

Just as I always surmised …

Nothing to do.

Nowhere to go.

Nothing to teach.

Shining the Light.

Being.

Here Now.

Huge pulsating vortex.

Spiralling bright colours.

Millions of doors.

Serene silence.

I choose.

* * *

Rain pelting against the window. Snaps me out of my reverie. The coffee-house is empty.

The Specials board has blown over. I hurry out to the sidewalk. Sudden gust of wind. A woman loses her umbrella and shouts in frustration.

No.

I choose.

Carry the Specials board inside. Stand by the huge glass door.

Gazing at the frenetic City activity. CEOs, stockbrokers, lawyers, bankers.

Where are they going in such a hurry?

Take a deep breath and resign from my job.

On the way home I notice a vacant store. It's a short walk from our apartment.

Make a phone call and organise a viewing.

Scrutinise and survey the premises.

Hmm ... this could work.

Arrive at the apartment.

Throw open the shutters. Sun is peeping through the clouds.

Glance at the to-do list.

Laugh happily.

I hear the front door.

Heart beating loudly in my chest.

"Angela!" I embrace her passionately.

"Ryana!" Relishing the adorable giggles.

Staring at them. Absorbing them. Holding them.

What can I say? They have no idea where I've been.

Soon the familiar routine. Bath duty. Cooking. Bedtime story.

Over a glass of wine I discuss my plan with Angela.

We have enough savings and business experience.

A decision is made.

Within two months the local store is refurbished.

Beautiful colour scheme. Beige and warm mocha.

Promotion, advertising and fanfare.

It's the opening of Cuppa Joe!

My own coffee-house.

* * *

Friends used to call me 'regular Joe'.

Now I have a new designation.

Some refer to me as 'Cuppa Joe'. Others hail me as 'barista'.

You wouldn't notice me. I am the guy who smiles at you in the morning as you order your fancy coffee. What will it be today? Caffè Americano? Caffè Latte? Caffè Mocha? Cappuccino? Espresso?

If you have a few moments ... place your order ... let me sprinkle a magic design upon your cappuccino. Perhaps a soaring eagle amid the swirling white foam ... a dolphin rendered from chocolate syrup and froth ... an inspiring phrase written with cocoa powder ...

The weeks go by. Business is good. I settle into my new life.

It is late afternoon. A soft sun is slowly disappearing behind the nearby buildings.

In strides a man with unkempt long dark hair, olive skin, unshaven. His long coat flares behind him.

I've heard you make award-winning cappuccinos.

"Michael!"

Beaming smile.

"What are you doing here?"

I have a fundamental question.

"Really?"

Yeah.

"Hang on."

I glance at his essence. Brew the cappuccino. Create a frothy design.

"Ok. What's the question?"

He gestures with his hand. *Why did you choose this?*

The door chime announces a new customer.

Bouncy long blonde hair ... ice-blue eyes ... curves in all the right places ... mmm ... that delicious scent mingled with soft lavender.

Angela.

"Hey honey, finished work early?"

She nods and unleashes the bundle of joy.

Pitter-patter of little feet. "Daddy. Daddy." My heart melts. "Ryana, sweetheart." I sweep my gorgeous two-year-old into my arms and hold her tight. Then I hoist her into the air and gaze into her eyes. She giggles playfully.

I notice Michael hesitate before sipping the cappuccino.

He sees the answer.

The miracle of Love.

I smile quietly.

Subdued shimmer denotes his goodbye.

Later we are locking up the coffee-house.

I have rented advertising space on a nearby wall.

On it reads the following:

'Cuppa Joe. Purveyor of Fine Coffee and Love.

Cherish your loved ones. Nurture your community. Find joy in the little things: The whisper of a gentle breeze, the sun on your skin, the smell of the ocean, the grass underfoot, a flower in your hair, a song in your heart, a butterfly in your hand.'

I put Ryana in the baby carriage and clasp Angela's hand.

Together we stroll along the tree-lined avenue toward our apartment.

We're going home.

Stephen Shaw's Books

Visit the website: www.i-am-stephen-shaw.com

I Am contains spiritual and mystical teachings from enlightened masters that point the way to love, peace, bliss, freedom and spiritual awakening.

Heart Song takes you on a mystical adventure into creating your reality and manifesting your dreams, and reveals the secrets to attaining a fulfilled and joyful life.

They Walk Among Us is a love story spanning two realities. Explore the mystery of the angels. Discover the secrets of Love Whispering.

The Other Side explores the most fundamental question in each reality. What happens when the physical body dies? Where do you go? Expand your awareness. Journey deep into the Mystery.

Reflections offers mystical words for guidance, meditation and contemplation. Open the book anywhere and unwrap your daily inspiration.

5D is the Fifth Dimension. Discover ethereal doorways hidden in the fabric of space-time. Seek the advanced mystical teachings.

Star Child offers an exciting glimpse into the future on earth. The return of the gods and the advanced mystical teachings. And the ultimate battle of light versus darkness.

The Tribe expounds the joyful creation of new Earth. What happened after the legendary battle of Machu Picchu? What is Christ consciousness? What is Ecstatic Tantra?

The Fractal Key reveals the secrets of the shamans. This handbook for psychonauts discloses the techniques and practices used in psychedelic healing and transcendent journeys.

CPSIA information can be obtained
at www.ICGtesting.com
Printed in the USA
BVHW062125080319
542134BV00002B/185/P